Another World Instead

THE EARLY POEMS OF

William Stafford

1937–1947

Prison Camp

~~Hard times in the laugh~~

~~Today~~

                   laugh

I heard the homeless ~~man laughing~~
I heard the prisoners sing
  I knew I couldn't leave my place with them
    for anything.

Across the yard and the grass
I saw those men and their friends got --
helpless, proud, deaf and blind with youth
like snow; --

Their lives a slanting toward earth
their passing a soft blur on the eye
white, white in the heart and on the hills
that snowflake, songflake, thoughtflake
             went by.

"Fellowship" June 4 '43
still considering
Winterset Oct. 10, '43

Another World Instead

The Early Poems of
William Stafford
1937–1947

Edited by Fred Marchant

Graywolf Press
SAINT PAUL, MINNESOTA

Publication of this volume is made possible in part by a grant provided by the Minnesota State Arts Board, through an appropriation by the Minnesota State Legislature; a grant from the Wells Fargo Foundation Minnesota; and a grant from the National Endowment for the Arts, which believes that a great nation deserves great art. Significant support has also been provided by the Bush Foundation; Target; the McKnight Foundation; and other generous contributions from foundations, corporations, and individuals. To these organizations and individuals we offer our heartfelt thanks.

Grateful acknowledgment is also made to the following publishers for permission to use selections from copyrighted materials.

An Anthology of Northwest Writing: 1900–1950. Edited by Michael Strelow. Northwest Review Books, 1979; reprinted by University of Oregon Press, 2003. *Down in My Heart: Peace Witness in War Time* by William Stafford. Originally published: Elgin, Illinois: Brethren Publishing House, 1947. Reprinted and published by Oregon State University Press, 2006, with Introduction by Kim Stafford. *Every War Has Two Losers: William Stafford on Peace and War.* Edited and with an Introduction by Kim Stafford. Milkweed Editions, 2003. *The Redress of Poetry* by Seamus Heaney. Farrar, Straus and Giroux, 1995. *A Scripture of Leaves* by William Stafford. Brethren Press, 1999. *Simone Weil: An Anthology.* Edited by Sian Miles. Grove Press, 1986. *Writing the Australian Crawl: Views on the Writer's Vocation* by William Stafford. The University of Michigan Press, 1978. *You Must Revise Your Life* by William Stafford. The University of Michigan Press, 1986.

Published by Graywolf Press
2402 University Avenue, Suite 203
Saint Paul, Minnesota 55114
All rights reserved.

www.graywolfpress.org

Published in the United States of America

ISBN 978-1-55597-497-8

2 4 6 8 9 7 5 3 1
First Graywolf Printing, 2008

Library of Congress Control Number: 2007925195

Cover design: Christa Schoenbrodt, Studio Haus
Cover photograph: Courtesy of the Estate of William Stafford

Contents

1946–1947

Introduction

What does it mean to be a conscientious objector during a war that nearly all one's fellow citizens favor? What does it mean to take such a stance at the same time that one is getting started as a poet? How does such an experience shape the poetry, and how does the poetry articulate the inner life of a person in such a situation?

Answers to such questions are not easy to come by. Most readers of William Stafford's poetry know that he was a CO during World War II. Most know that he spent the war years in the Civilian Public Service program, doing alternative service that consisted of forestry and soil-conservation projects. Some may have read *Down in My Heart* (1947), Stafford's prose memoir about his time in the CPS program. It details the lives of men who were opposed to war, but were essentially conscripted into a program governed by the Selective Service System. As important as *Down in My Heart* is, it is not, however, a portrait of the artist as a young man. While Stafford uses poems he wrote in that era as epigraphs for several of his chapters in the memoir, there is very little in the book about his coming of age as a writer. *Down in My Heart* focuses on the ethical dilemmas these men often faced by virtue of their convictions, and if anything, the seven poems in the memoir are supplemental to those stories. In addition to those in the memoir, there are only nine other poems from those years that are readily available to contemporary readers. Three are collected in *The Way It Is* (1998), Stafford's posthumously published new and selected poems. Two can be found in *Early Morning* (2002), Kim Stafford's memoir about his father. Another two are collected in *Every War Has Two Losers* (2003), an anthology of Stafford's writings on war and peace, edited by Kim Stafford. The remaining two poems are in *An Anthology of Northwest Writing: 1900–1950* (first published in 1979, and reprinted in 2003).

These sixteen poems, however, are only a small fraction of the writing Stafford did while in the CPS program and the years shortly after his discharge. The William Stafford Archives in Portland, Oregon, contain approximately four hundred poems composed between 1937 and 1947. Not all of them, of course, are of equal worth, and some are clearly in the spirit of daily note-taking and ongoing practice. A surprising number of these poems, however, are fully realized, and utterly fascinating, but unavailable in print. The present volume collects 176 poems from Stafford's first four hundred, including those that are still in print. The goal has been to assemble a representative and accurate record of Stafford's best work from his first decade of writing. An even more significant goal is to allow these poems to tell the developmental story that they embody. When *West of Your City,* Stafford's first book of poetry, was published in 1960, the poet was forty-six years old. To many, Stafford seemed to spring full-grown onto the American literary scene, but that accomplished style did have a background story. If Stafford didn't exactly have an apprenticeship, in the strict sense of that word, he nonetheless had had a long period of getting started as a writer. He had been writing poems for over twenty years before his first book was published. The central event of his life in the first of those two decades was his service in the CPS program. Despite their hardships, those four years were their own blessing in disguise. They were the crucible in which Stafford forged the basic elements of his distinctive poetic voice.

The poems that follow show us Stafford seeking to understand the full meaning involved in his taking a stance against war. This was deep, inner-life work, and was in its way as demanding as his daily physical labor. In May 1942, Stafford was in the CPS work camp in Los Prietos, California, in the mountains above Santa Barbara. He had been in the system only a few months, but they were enough to make him feel as if he was living as an exile within his own country. In that frame of mind, Stafford wrote a poem titled "Exile," containing this quatrain:

I stand and dream another world instead,
where easy wind flows river over head,

and quail call outdoor reverence through the day,
and men look far to cove and sheen blue bay.

The stateliness of the first line shows his devotion to the ceremonial quality of iambic pentameter, but the whole stanza is awkward, especially the last line. One wonders what Stafford means. Is it that he wishes he were anywhere else but here? Is this a vain and idle dream?

Six months later, while still working at the same camp, Stafford revisits the question in another, far more complex and accomplished poem, "CO's Work on Mountain Road," quoted here in full:

Like bay trees on the edge of La Cumbre Peak,
liking with wistful scent the swooping world below,
    we few dreamers
on the edge of new savage years, jagged beyond sight,
audaciously lean, suspiring a few old messages from
    the old earth still under our trustful feet.
The pines have left us and are marching;
the sycamores fly angry tints;
the oaks present overworked postures, extreme.
Who cares in a big country for a few egret trees,
    on one cliff, on an edge, leaning far out,
    on a scent like a memory?

Who would care in such a big country, in a world at war, about a few people who have put themselves so far out on the margins of society? Why should anyone care? And yet the poem proposes that, like the bay trees, these COs and their work serve a purpose nonetheless. The poem implies their work offers the angry world below something precious and needed. Like these trees, the COs breathe a sweetness over the landscape. These few dreamers working on the road cling to the ancient injunction: thou shalt not kill. To keep that idea or faith alive is the real work of COs up there in the mountains. This is the fuller version of the dream of another world instead.

If Stafford in his first few months in the CPS program wondered what it meant to be a conscientious objector, he also might have wondered what good it was to write poetry. Though many years later, Seamus Heaney nonetheless examines the same question in *The Redress of Poetry*, when he analyzes the concept of a "poetry of witness." Heaney argues that a poem may bear witness in a variety of ways, and that the act of witnessing can be more complex than a simple reportorial account. The pressure of reality may prompt a poet to imagine a world in which there is "a glimpsed alternative" to what is often the savagery of the real. He observes that a poem of witness might reveal "a potential that is denied or constantly threatened." Heaney also notes that a poem might place in the scales a "counter-reality," an image that allows us to see better both what is and what is missing from it. For Heaney the "redress" of poetry is its capacity to amplify and extend our conception of existence. To do this work is less an idle dream and more of an effort to help forge, as Joyce says, the uncreated conscience of a people. On that mountain road Stafford forged images that bore witness to and affirmed the worth of the two fundamental facts of his life: his pacifist's stance and his writing of poetry. For him the two were then and would remain inseparable for the rest of his life.

Stafford was born in Hutchinson, Kansas, on January 17, 1914. The oldest of three children, he came of age during the Great Depression, the family moving from town to town as his father tried to secure work during the hard times. The family's religious background was a mainstream Protestantism. Stafford recalled going regularly to various Sunday schools, though the family had no firm denominational affiliation. In Kansas of that era, Stafford may have had some exposure to Mennonites and members of other historic peace churches. He also may have gathered some useful skepticism from his family's common-sense distrust of war-mongering political leaders. His family, however, was not a pacifist family. Stafford's brother Bob, for instance, became a bomber pilot during World War II, and the family supported both young men. Moreover, Bob and Bill seemed genuinely concerned about the well-being of each throughout the war years despite their divergent paths. In short, what Stafford seems to have absorbed from his family background was a sturdy, almost Emersonian self-reliance.

One sign of this self-reliance is that while an undergraduate at the University of Kansas in the late 1930s, Stafford became a member of the Fellowship of Reconciliation. This pacifist organization, begun in England prior to World War I, had a thriving American branch at the university. Though originally organized by Christians, the Fellowship was ecumenical, committed to social justice, and to nonviolence as a response to conflict. During World War I, it supported conscientious objectors in all the warring countries. In the United States, it not only worked for legal recognition of CO rights, it also helped organize the National Civil Liberties Bureau, which later became the American Civil Liberties Union. Peaceful reconciliation of conflict seems to have emerged as Stafford's core ethical belief during his college years. In one of his prose writings there is a brief account of his taking part in a nonviolent demonstration to desegregate the university's cafeteria. His participation in that demonstration might well be representative of his overall frame of mind in response to Depression-era America. Stafford began his university studies as an economics major, but graduated with a degree in English, and later began work on a master's degree, while planning on teaching.

In the fall of 1941, as war loomed, Stafford applied to his draft board for conscientious objector status. At his hearing, he was asked how he came by his objection to war. The questioner was the head of Stafford's draft board, but he also had been one of Stafford's Sunday school teachers. Stafford replied that he had come to his stance because people such as his questioner had taught him not to kill. It was a lesson, he said, "I never forgot." He was telling the truth. "White Pigeons," written in 1937, was his first poem, as indicated by Stafford's own notation on the typescript. In this piece a boy in a desolate landscape is startled by a strange sound in the sky above. We learn that the boy's white pigeons are returning to him. Whatever the exact kind of pigeons these are, they cannot help but evoke the doves that represent peace. The situation in the poem seems surrounded by important questions. Is the sound in the air only the sound of the pigeons? Have they been frightened by the screeching of a bird of prey? The answers are not evident, but the poem is colored by feelings of dread and loneliness, the bird-sounds presenting what the young poet calls the "haunting cry of aching land."

Another poem that reflected the sincerity and self-reliance involved in his stance was "From the Sound of Peace." This was composed in the fall of 1941, around the time when Stafford made his claim for CO status to his draft board. In this poem the speaker also hears a sound high in the air, and this poem too is filled with dread. What this speaker hears is a prophetic voice calling us all back from the brink of war. The speaker in this poem would like nothing better than to preserve some shred of peace in the face of an imminent onslaught. He damns those who follow the lying voices calling for war. One can easily imagine a poem like this being offered as evidence that he had never forgotten that first lesson about not killing. He was granted CO status, and a few months later, shortly after the attack on Pearl Harbor, Stafford's draft notice arrived. In January 1942 Stafford said goodbye to his family and left for a Civilian Public Service work camp near Magnolia, Arkansas. He would serve in the program for four full years, and would be discharged six months after the war ended.

The Civilian Public Service program was a creation of the Selective Service Act of 1940. The CPS provision of the legislation was in no small part due to a collaborative effort among the historic peace churches, including the Friends, the Mennonites, and the Church of the Brethren. The churches were responding to the brutal difficulties COs faced during World War I, both within the military and within federal prisons. Given the social turbulence of the Depression era, these church officials expected a wave of war resisters should another world war break out. The U.S. government also anticipated resistance, and the Selective Service System, led by General Lewis B. Hershey, worked with the peace churches to design an alternative service program. Thus was born a program where COs could do "work of national importance" under civilian direction. The program's enabling legislation had specified that the program would be under civilian control, but after Pearl Harbor, the Selective Service claimed absolute authority over the program, and given the wartime atmosphere, there was no practical way for the peace churches to challenge the claim. The Selective Service, with the blessing of President Roosevelt, seemed to view the conscientious objector as a variety of draftee and the peace churches as a source of funding and administrative services for the camps.

The CPS program consisted of approximately 150 work camps scattered across the country. The men would be paid from funds raised by those churches, and thus the program was designed to cost the government little or no money. That was one of the selling points in the creation of the program. Some 34 million men registered for the draft during World War II. Approximately 72,000 applied for CO status. A third of those failed the physical and were exempted from service. Another third accepted noncombatant status within the military, often serving as medics. Roughly 6,000 men did not cooperate with the draft at all, and thus were arrested, tried, and sentenced to jail terms of varying lengths. Approximately 12,000 conscientious objectors declared themselves unwilling to serve in the military in a noncombatant role, but were willing to do alternative service in the CPS program.

Stafford was one of these men. As he waited for the train to take him to Magnolia, he might have imagined what his immediate future would be like from the list of items he had been instructed to bring with him: denim work clothes, sturdy boots, long underwear, bed linens, shoe polish, and a mirror. It would be demanding, physical work in the wilderness. He and others like him would live in barracks and buildings built for the Depression-era Civilian Conservation Corps. It might have been a little reassuring for him to note that "literature supplies" and "stationery and stamps" were on his list of things to bring as well. Even so, aside from the fact that the COs of Civilian Public Service were so small a number, Stafford might easily have felt as if he was heading off to a pacifist's boot camp.

All COs were to stay in the CPS program for the duration of the war.

Leaves had to be authorized. To go AWOL was a criminal violation. The pay was $2.50 per month, far less than the lowest private in any service. Day-to-day life in the camps was to be as much like garrison army life as possible. Work reports and disciplinary actions went up a chain of command, and weekend passes and the occasional furloughs were tightly regulated. If one overstayed a pass or leave, one was AWOL; if one deliberately left and did not intend to return, he was in effect a deserter and could be arrested by the FBI. The regimentation and the miserable pay after a while seemed to resemble something more or less akin to forced labor, designed to keep COs out of sight and out of mind. As the war went on, more and more CPS men did take a principled stance against the program and deserted as an act of civil disobedience.

Those who stayed often had to endure the havoc their CPS work wreaked upon their families. Making pennies per day, they had to rely on donations from the peace churches to support wives and children back home. Especially onerous was the indeterminate length of the "sentence" these men felt had been imposed upon them. Sometimes, a CO might give up and enlist in the army just to get a decent paycheck to send some money back to loved ones. And those who could put up with the financial and physical hardships often found themselves wondering whether they were being altogether too compliant with a war machine they had opposed.

For Stafford, staying within the Civilian Public Service may have made good ethical sense, but it had its personal costs. Stafford's father died in September, 1943, while the poet was in the Los Prietos camp in California. In the aftermath Stafford obtained an emergency leave to return to Kansas to help out his mother, who, because of emotional distress, had been briefly hospitalized. Not all was misery at Los Prietos, and aside from the comradeship, there was one significant surprise. Because the camp was administered by the Church of the Brethren, a local Brethren minister visited one Sunday afternoon in the spring of 1943, bringing with him his daughter, Dorothy Hope Frantz. A year later she and William Stafford married, and for the rest of the war years they were able to visit frequently, beginning a marriage that would last until the poet's death in 1993.

The world meanwhile kept spiraling in a lethal nightmare. In the month that Stafford arrived at Magnolia, the Nazi leadership gathered at Wannsee to discuss the "final solution" of the "Jewish question." A year later, while Stafford was at the Los Prietos camp, the Allied leadership met at Casablanca to agree on area bombing of cities, leading to massive civilian casualties in Berlin, Dresden, Tokyo, and eventually in the use of the atom bomb in Hiroshima and Nagasaki. One cannot be sure exactly how much news of the war reached the CPS camps in the wilderness, but every CPS member recounts that the off-hours were usually times of intense discussion, study, and artistic expression. In many camps a portion of the barracks would be set off as a library. Books would be pooled, and those who had some special expertise would lead discussion groups. Musicians would practice, and writers would write. There would be readings and dramatic presentations. Descriptions of the off-hours at these CPS camps make them sound more than a little like free universities rather than work camps. It was in the spirit of conscientious objection—whether on philosophical or religious grounds—that the important, difficult questions would come under intense and probing scrutiny.

For Stafford, the most valuable off-hours in the day were early morning. Rising at 4:30, he had a couple of hours before breakfast and the workday began. The Selective Service System did not own those early mornings, and those were the hours when he wrote. In an autobiographical essay written later in life and included in *You Must Revise Your Life* (1986), Stafford explained that his life as a writer came to him as two parts, "like two rivers that blend." The first consisted of times, places, events, and people. The other, he said, was the mysterious "flow of my inner life." Later in the same essay he recalled that in the camps "the two parts of my life that blended or clashed in making my writing were in constant alertness." Moreover he said that his daily writing early in the morning was "maintenance work or repair work on my integrity." Thus began his lifelong habit of rising early and writing before the day began for everyone else. There is probably no more important fact about Stafford's writing life than this daily habit, and one cannot help but imagine that he often remembered when and where that habit had begun.

The prison-like regimentation of life must have felt like an assault on his integrity. Even his cooperation with the authorities might have felt that way as well. To write in the free hours of the early morning might have been his best antidote to a pervasive sense of violation and vulnerability. In such a context the freedom to experiment in writing a poem would then be more than a technical matter. Trying out free verse or the many possibilities of indentations might have been deeply restorative. The poems of those years tell us he experimented with capitalization, punctuation, and syntax, with colloquial diction, with full rhymes, slant-rhymes, and none. Most of the characteristic elements of his style were discovered or invented—sometimes very tentatively—in the poems of these years. There are, however, surprising dimensions as well. These often are tonal or attitudinal gestures. Sometimes he is wickedly sarcastic, recoiling from specious piety, whatever its source, including overly pious pacifists and reformers. Other times he is so deeply alienated that it seems fair to say that Stafford's early poems were an ongoing investigation into loneliness. At the same time, Stafford is acutely aware of the benefits of being part of a beloved community, being a "saint of the kingdom," as the COs jokingly sometimes called themselves. In these poems the loneliness predominates, but the *communitas* among his fellow COs would remain for Stafford a benchmark of human possibility.

Above all, time and time again the work of Stafford's first decade of poetry enacts his visceral recoil from the pervasive violence of world war. One of the best examples is a poem he wrote on August 8, 1945, in between the bombing of Hiroshima and that of Nagasaki. "The Sound: Summer, 1945," quoted here in its entirety:

Not a loud sound, the buzz of the rattlesnake.
But urgent. Making the heart pound a loud drum.

Somewhere in dead weeds by a dry lake
On cracked earth flat in the sun.

The living thing left raises the fanged head,
Tormented and nagged by the drouth,
And stares past a planet that's dead,
With anger and death in its mouth.

When this poem was written, Stafford was serving in the administrative headquarters of the Church of the Brethren, in Elgin, Illinois, having been transferred there in the winter of 1945. He was no longer laboring in the mountains fighting forest fires and opening roads, but doing administrative work in the education programs for the Brethren CPS camps. No doubt he had seen enough newspaper photographs of the smoke from bombs to think the atomic bomb would have smoke that rose like a snake from its target. Still, one cannot help but marvel at Stafford's instinctive recognition that the rising "mushroom cloud" was the embodiment of an evil that threatened the whole planet. There is palpable revulsion, and no small amount of anger and fear, emotions one might not often associate with Stafford's poetry. Nevertheless, what is true of this poem points in the direction of the most fundamental and original element of his art.

A first principle: there is no essentially pacifist poetic. No line break, no figure of speech, no cadence is by its very nature pacifistic. A second principle: a pacifist poet cannot help but make aesthetic decisions that reflect or embody a core set of beliefs. To illustrate, let us reconsider "White Pigeons," Stafford's first poem, and this time take a close look at one of the oddities in the poem: its use of the dash. Four lines of the opening stanza's seven lines end on a dash. The second stanza is slightly longer, and no dashes interrupt the flow. The concluding stanza, however, repeats the first, including its four dashes in seven lines. Stafford's reliance on the em-dash is not in any way unique to this poem. The posthumous new and selected poems of *The Way It Is* are certainly representative of Stafford's life's work. It turns out that nearly half of them have sentences that are interrupted by dashes. For Stafford it is one the most versatile elements of punctuation that exists: he uses it to indicate asides, explanations, pauses, hesitations, and sudden shifts in thought. It is a device that alters not only the forward thrust of syntax, but also the temporal dimension of the poem. It creates silences as much as it creates interruptions and delays. It dramatizes the mind lingering, where the speaker is momentarily open to something that is imminent but not yet fully articulate. It is no wonder then that Stafford should have said, as he did in an interview included in *Writing the Australian Crawl* (1978), that there was no American writer then at work who was greater than Emily Dickinson. She and Stafford were both virtuosos of the dash.

The most famous dashes in Stafford's work occur in the oft-anthologized "Traveling through the Dark." The dead doe encountered on a wilderness road at night proves to have a fetus still alive inside. What is he supposed to do? Stafford tells us:

> I thought hard for us all—my only swerving—,
> then pushed her over the edge into the river.

These dashes surround and enable the speaker's mindful moment. They are the sign and symbol of his swerving from the forward, inevitable thrust of thought and logic. In this regard one is reminded of another pacifist writer during World War II, Simone Weil. In "The *Iliad*, or the Poem of Force," an essay written during the first year of World War II, Weil celebrates the virtues of hesitation, pausing, swerving. Examining several blood-stained scenes in the poem, she notes that those who conquer and kill—be they Greek or Trojan—are inexorable. No one imposes the slightest halt in what they are doing. No one, she writes, insists on "that interval of hesitation, wherein lies all our consideration for our brothers in humanity." For Stafford, the dash—a mute little shred of punctuation—was the syntactical device that signaled the speaker was, as he said in his most well-known poem, thinking hard for us all.

Stafford's dashes are but one device by which his poetry creates the interval of hesitation. There are parentheses and ellipsis points that work the same way. But it is not always a matter of punctuation. Or rather the punctuation is but a sign of what Stafford considers a fundamental human act of attentiveness: listening. Throughout the poems selected for *The Way It Is* there are listeners listening and bearing witness to that topic as Stafford's abiding concern. It is central to the early work as well. In the poems of his first decade Stafford listens to sounds in the air, to voices in the night, to winds, to trees, to the kind of men who lecture or pronounce, and to the kind who love to sing. In 1946 Stafford composed "Deep Listening," a philosophical poem in which he tries to pinpoint with metaphor what exactly listening means for him. First the speaker says deep listening is like a taut wire humming before it snaps; then he says it is like a creaking chain about to break. Then the poem shifts to a surprisingly active set of images:

> I watch an oak whose top
>   has forgotten the ground under the leaves.
> At the final swing of the axe
>   the high branches glisten,
>   whisper, then lean
>   with surging recognition
>   to an old friend.
>
> I turn to you
>   and listen.

To think that listening to another deeply is akin to an oak being felled suggests just how seriously Stafford views the question. To listen is like returning to the ground of one's own being. The tree falls, and dies, and the kind of listening Stafford describes here implies giving oneself over fully to another. Hearing has a somewhat passive connotation; deep listening, as Stafford presents it, is a profoundly active turning toward. It is a "listing," that leaning, that cocking of the ear, that pause in which one allows for authentic consideration of the other. It is a paradigm of mindful human connectedness, and it is the archetypal act underlying Stafford's poetry.

In his first decade of writing, and in particular in the four years he spent in the CPS program, William Stafford discovered that writing poetry was for him an act of deep listening. He was not only listening to the voices in his world. He was also listening inwardly, to signals emanating from the deepest levels of his own being. One name for that would be a conscience. One might think conscience is a purely individual matter. Yet the structure of the word tells us differently. Conscience is a "knowing-with." It acknowledges the importance of the other. It proposes that we find or create a sense of right relation with one another, with the world around us, and with ourselves. How can one know what those right relations are? Stafford might answer by saying one has to learn how to listen deeply. In the poems he wrote between 1937 and 1947, we witness Stafford learning how to do just that. In later years he would write a poem about when he first met his muse. When she appeared the ceiling of his house arched, the sunlight bent, and her voice "belled forth":

> "I am your own
> way of looking at things," she said. "When
> you allow me to live with you, every
> glance at the world around you will be
> a sort of salvation."

Stafford ends this poem by saying that then he took her hand. He was listening to what she had to say, listening deeply.

Fred Marchant

Another World Instead

For Poems—'42 and '43

I carry pieces of my world before the crowd.
When I drop them everyone hears.
I put them together, but they are not the same.
I take them back. I pick them up and take them home.
All I have—everything I have—are the wonderful shine of two years,
And pieces of a different world.

Los Prietos, California
May 5, 1944

1937—1941

White Pigeons

What's that—
The trumpet call, the haunting cry of aching land—
A wild goose passing?
From down what violet sky—
The looming winter sky now edging frozen land—
Come circling home
White pigeons?

This is the aching land,
The bleak and desolate.
This is the plains.
On this blank loneliness in huddled clump
A house, a barn, and fences.
A boy, foreshortened, small, wind-buffeted,
His pigeons watched come home.
Hard sky, hard earth.
Soft pigeons.
Grateful pigeons, rustling, sleepy cluttering.
Soft
Soft pigeons.

What's that!—
The trumpet call, the haunting cry of aching land—
A wild goose passing?
From down what violet sky—
The looming winter night now edging frozen land—
Come circling home
White pigeons?

Lawrence, Kansas
Spring 1937

To Schumann-Heink

Too near the heart, the lullaby, too near,
The strains it trolls are melting twisting strains;
You should not sing the song for us to hear,
For pains it soothes away bring sadder pains.

The pulse of sorrow vibrates all alone,
And when the grandeur of the voice that's gone
Reflects an instant in the shaking tone,
What sudden memories to light are drawn.

Your love has been so great, your life so long,
That feeling in your voice is like a dart,
And when you think far back and sing the song,
You stab too near the heart, too near the heart.

El Dorado, Kansas
c. Fall 1938

Purpose

Not ask for eloquence, for tongues of men
When loosed forget the falseness that creeps in
When force usurps the place of honesty.
Of thunder-truth I would speak casually,
And watch that star, belief, grow bright and rise
Across the warm horizon of your eyes.

Lawrence, Kansas
c. March 1941

Subject and Background

No matter, add a wrinkle, add a scowl:
I see the baby head behind it all;
And see bewilderment suppressed and hid
In gray temples upon the wisest head;
See comically the great men prance and caper,
And strike poses, and treble threats at neighbors.
Meanwhile, the background: the judge-quiet skies;
The canyon-maimed mountains; the stanchless days.

Lawrence, Kansas
c. March 1941

Communication from a Wanderer

"I will become a pilgrim
And walk as wide as all the world lasteth . . ."

I. REPORT OF KANSAS IN WINTER

(To everyone passed in the crowd whose eyes said hello:
    yes, he saw you.
To those hurt by the deeds and the talk every day:
    it hurt him too.
To all who hinted what pride or convention or fear wouldn't
    let them say:
    he heard you; he was there with you.
To whoever are wondering if he gets their hopes, fears,
    insinuations:
    he does.
He does from being winter-homeless in Kansas.)

This is the high steppes of Siberia in his mind.
This is where the lonesomeness of the world shoulders in and stands.
This is to walk on a frozen dead street in a strange town,
    and there in the graveyard night by the railroad yards,
    and the cold steel wind, and the pitted cement of that doorway
    to lay a life down.
And they robbed him there in the secret ways, the bandits,
    the ones with the final grasp on exhibit A, the swag.
They held him up with their cruel weird pistols—
    the camouflaged ways of forcing the victim down.

II. REPORT OF THE NATIONAL FOREST

    (No more alone, listening, in the night.
    Quiet, the jeweled brook sparkles back the stealthy star.
    Quick with pain the owl cries
        drift above snow-silent passes
        more wool than sleep, more white than sudden fear.
    No more along.)

He heard the owl cries in the long night there
    go undulating through the muffled night,
    and heard the multitude of trees go, proud,
    moon-elegant, go, white-leaved votaries,
    to swan their limbs before the steady sound
    of air-surf loose in sky-tranced limbs above.
He saw the skeletons of cliffs in agonies
    of beauty by the moon, and one lone star
    riding an ice-torn wind by frozen peaks,
    and all the vacant hollow sky a rushing
    sound—escaping night pouring enormous coils
    of lean hard air out toward the far and cold
    of unknown space and writhing forest sea.

He saw contorted land, an epileptic
    held rigid in the dark, awed by the sky,
    a blind and clumsy giant stumbling through
    a hazy star-smoke curtain billowing
    in eon watch ticks, a world they never have
    bound yet within the scrapbook minds of men.

III. REPORT OF THE SOUTHWEST

    (Trees on a hill in the sun!
    The cry of yellow sunsets beyond Las Vegas.
    A slowly-over tumbleweed on an empty street.
    The sudden lift as a clumsy hawk leaves tame ground
        and with piercing beauty wing-hovers
        in a free wind.)

This is the tangy land of wide, strong, sunlit places.
Drums beat here under the earth, then silence.
The air fermented, tart; the sky tight.
Here the days flow, cliffs in the honey-sun.
Here he would stand by the far-apart trees looking out
    and the wind blowing, here where the days breathe grass, drip
        flowers.
The friends here have sultry eyes, are dangerous people.
They have the dark strangeness in their minds, the suddenness.
The ears yearn in this land for the wild tunes.
There is no rest, for the rich world curves endlessly on.
The taste of tomorrow always on the tongue,
    and the strange unrest.
And a flavor of lost uncaught stampeding time,
    and lawless eyes, and wild hosts in the mind.

    (Who have only the hunger
      and not the means—
       the fingers clenching, the slow-turning head,
       the eyes far-wanting, but the hope not there—
    these are the men he will speak in silent air.)

Armed with the eyes, he marched across their land;
    and calm he stood alone, and arrogant,
    his hair the wind's way, there upon the sand
    that grovels to the stumbling waves aslant
    like white wings on the slobbering, bullying sea.
The eyes, caged up for armament till then,
    roamed out across that eye-wide prison, free—
    but soon by the horizon trapped again.
No longer stern, the laughter loose in his head,
    the warm rain falling on his back, he turned,
    the whole world softly turning, visions dead,
    and nothing left but this that he had learned:
Pilgrims turn back from what they can't quite see
    and seek in caves the blind for company.

Lawrence, Kansas
c. May 1941

From the Sound of Peace

Now is glass and an egg and gossamer in the wind.
Tomorrow is darkness and a bomb ticking.
But peace and yesterday are a still pool.
Peace and yesterday are a shadow quiet on the wall.

And from the sound of peace I heard a voice,
A man who raised before the wind of steel
A wispy tapestry of wondering:

"Why follow half-way saviors, men who kill
Or lie or compromise for distant ends?
Marauders come; but no man dares cry 'Wolf!'
The wolves look too much like our guardians.

"Why call disaster wrapped in cellophane
On all our streets, and beautiful destruction
In all our books, and plays—and sermons, too?
Why laugh at those who seek Utopia?
We send heroes to die impeccably,
Genteelly, for tomorrow, for some day
When saviors need not be crucified.

"Can our fierce-Christian eyes still hope to see
A glad, redemption, miracle third-day?
An angel with a flaming sword on guard?
For, see on tombs of all our saviors—stones,
Unmoved, and big, and still—We put them there."

I saw the listeners as the steel wind came on.
I saw their serious faces, in the dark,
In the night,
By shadow-fled lightning.
I saw their serious faces lifted in questioning silence
To night-plunging rain—
The shadowy eyes, the poignant throats . . . .

My place is only a little place, lost behind fronds,
Hidden in the wolf reaches of the terrible earth.
And mine is only a little cry from a huddled black figure,
Stunned by grandeur, on a windy quay,
In the limitless rage of a dawn;
But out of the sickness of a haunting vision
I would cry a wall for them—
For the storm-awakened people, in the dark, in the night,
In the rain.

Lawrence, Kansas
c. October 1941

Discovery [I]

One day, turning, unresting in mountain sunlight,
I opened a valley over a rampart of warm tan stone—
Stone, stone, stone, softer and softer into the haze.
Tumultuous hills pouring down on me,
With steps just right I went on
(The thin warbling of the hills might escape,
easily, in a tinkle of air-sound),
and concentrated on the time, neglecting the rocks of the hill.
Then, safe now beyond the windless range
Below the strong deep day,
In the soundless torrent of green hills,
Knowing the truth, clutching the prize of my new-found dream,
Falling stumbling, wild with the sound of ear,
The sight of eye, the feel of air,
I crawled on soaring earth, safe

To the long far purple and life of the windless range:—
Learning to jar not the rapt thought, bruise not the mood,
Lose all the monuments, keep the thought-gold.

Lawrence, Kansas
Fall 1941

Home Town

Peace on my little town, a speck in the safe,
    comforting, impersonal immensity of Kansas.

Benevolence like a gentle haze on its courthouse
    (the model of Greek pillars to me)
    on its quiet little bombshell of a library,
    on its continuous, hidden, efficient sewer system.

Sharp, amazed, steadfast regard on its more upright citizenry,
    my nosy, incredible, delicious neighbors.

Haunting invasion of a train whistle to my friends,
    moon-gilding, regular breaths of the old memories to them—
    the old whispers, old attempts, old beauties, ever new.

Peace on my little town, haze-blessed, sun-friended,
    dreaming sleepy days under the world-champion sky.

Lawrence, Kansas
c. Fall 1941

Women of Kansas

Mother, Grandmother—women in early Kansas—
Lived under a shawl,
Hurried from house to barn,
Stood looking across plain,
Raised solemn eyes to cloud—
Held their heads in the home of a shawl,
A shred of home held close.
Women in that world fluttered between houses,
Wore shawls.

Lawrence, Kansas
c. Fall 1941

Observation

surprisingly harsh & judgmental

Bending over, watching them quietly:—
They walk seriously and try to do things right.
They fit keys into locks on the second or third try.
They drive carefully, backing, and killing the engine, and trying again.
They hold napkins beneath their glasses.
They speak often and then go back saying "I mean . . . ."
They go feeling, fumbling forward into the days.

But they never go back and start over on the big things.
They never know they have fumbled life.
The whole ship and tenement of their lives moves on like the sun.

El Dorado, Kansas
December 1941

Choosing the long line means having to fill out extra words

1942—1945

At Roll Call

One day I stood, small shoes upon the sand,
and looked across a park through frozen trees;
the thorn and sky drove through my soul;
a whistle blew; I heard the end of things.

They told me while I stood, suddenly alone,
looking over the earth, not knowing what to say:
"Nostalgia," they said, "nostalgia,
a feeling men have; you will know it, later,
all your life . . . at dawn, at dusk, in mist . . .
you and all men, lost, even in the sun's brightness."

Today I stood alone among the men;
a whistle blew . . . the thorn and sky . . . .
"Nostalgia," they said, "nostalgia."

Magnolia, Arkansas
c. March 1942

Event

At evening on Feb. 26, the long flat sunlight,
The wistful wind silvering the marsh grass,
All the sleepy continent
(The many silent trees, the owls calling,
One shy fox with small feet on the pine needles
On a quiet knoll)
All the faint flavors of history
(Long smooth hours in Arabia,

The gum fragrance, the slow smoke loving the air)
Touched quaintly in Jake Martin, imperceptibly
(The kiss of two bubbles in brook foam)
With spring
(A hint of it, a thought of a breath of it)
At the cheep of a bird on a low limb
In the north pasture.

Magnolia, Arkansas
c. March 1942

A Vine

Slash thought and a thunder of miles distant
Forever south where the sky-weary tern
Steeply dives to rest in his flight
There in a land big as an endless dream
Steam-jungled, with mountain forest
And evermore, evermore hush
Is a mesa plateau, cliffed off alone.
And over the anxious stillness of deepest gulf
A giant tree prouds up, a limb crawls out
And there in the quiet over the cliff loneliness
Reaching eagerly a vine touches, mesa to tree.
In the desolation of not-knowing I have brushed the silence,
And have called this poem A Vine.

Magnolia, Arkansas
c. March 1942

Buzzards over Arkansas

Three somber wheeling buzzards tantalize a vortex
   invisible above a continent of pine cliffs
   and brush canyons.
Casual denim-tiger, a man walks a far lane
   toward casual supper.
Hog liver? Squirrel? The body of a soft rabbit?
Far down in a gulf of thought spins Arkansas.
The sun goes down. The fur sound of winter
   stifles the hurt mind.

Magnolia, Arkansas
c. March 1942

Inspirational Talk

"We must dedicate our lives!" The speaker views
The men all smothered in the muffling phrase.
"Give, give, be hurt, even to death!" he says.
Teasing his guilt with candy soldiers use.

Without this hate-called-love for human kin,
I meanwhile lolling in amoral ease
From loud guilt-frenzied saints take refugees—
Find little truth-flowers growing in my sin.

Magnolia, Arkansas
March 1942

Escape

With runaway wild smoke across the brain,
The weary geese fly on, the brown elk run,
The salmon fight the stream. The sound of rain
Falls curtains across thought, and I could run
Far to forever end with nothing but the blood
To tell me why in drum drum of the heart
And nothing to go toward but drum, blood, dream.

Magnolia, Arkansas
Spring 1942

Artist

"Men store their carefulness in things—
A picture, a book, a bit of ground,"
The quick man said, waving his hands there by the park.

I put my carefulness (a small book with words in ink)
On the grass by the bench and listened
To the man careless of his carefulness.

But he walked away, leaving me an idea:
The moving relaxed feel, the big art work
Your house, your job, your daily expression is.

Magnolia, Arkansas
April 1942

CO Park Project

On vehement-green Southern sod,
In vital blue dress a girl walks, and tries
Ten religious men, with a distant nod.
(Tongues move, heads rise, hoes hesitate.)
Ten dangerous men fail, pasture their eyes,
Turn dirt for the glory of God,
and wait.

Magnolia. Arkansas
April 1942

Friend Sky

Blue, blue forever ever and ever falling
(over the street I walk toward home)
Resting upon my eyes resting
(I have lived here all my life)
Soft over the trees over the hills
(I meet a man who hates me; he speaks curtly)
Over his shoulder soaring curving upswelling
(my house greets me; I enter the pleasant rooms)
Carrying the gaze forever and ever the sky.

Magnolia, Arkansas
April 1942

"Their voices were stilled . . ."

Their voices were stilled across the land.
I sought them. I listened.
The only voices were war voices.
Where are the others? I asked, lonely
      in the lush desert.
One voice told me secretly:
We do not speak now, lest we be misunderstood.
We cannot speak without awaking the dragon of anger
      to more anger still.
That is why you are lonely.
You must learn stillness now.

I looked into his eyes, and they were a dragon's eyes,
      and I could not speak,
And we were as grains of sand huddled under the wind,
Awaiting to be molded, waiting to persuade with yielding
      the feet of the dragon.

Magnolia, Arkansas
May 1, 1942

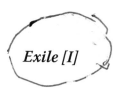

Exile [I]

In this gray pine-held land of furtive eyes
and captured kneeling hills, where whimsy dies,
where men fear other men, and fear to know,
where laughter of near friends is cruelest foe—

In this plow-battered land, clay insolent—
fire-shattered forest, ragged and wind-rent,
where valiant on the clay the grass is dry,
where men-beasts carry wood and fear the sky—

I stand and dream another world instead,
where easy wind flows river over head,
and quail call outdoor reverence through the day,
and men look far to cove and sheen blue bay.

Friends, gravely wise, I want to want to sing
(but know men's needs and live remembering).
If I had leave, I'd soon address trail sand—
and speak with lisping feet about this land.

Magnolia, Arkansas
May 1942

Exile [II]

The burning city of my sorrow hurts
And blinds the eye turned carelessly on it.
Avert the face; look full on it at night;
Be wary days. Increase the time of gaze
As time goes by, and hate grows strong,
And sight grows dim, and cities burn and die.

Magnolia, Arkansas
[1942]

The Prisoner

Touched the walls on every side again—
Obsessed with prowling thoughts of free live men.
He heard when guards had slammed the outer gates,
How suddenly like wool the silence waits.
Resigned, he sat and thought of all the dead.
"I'll soon wake up from life," the prisoner said.

c. Magnolia, Arkansas
[1942]

Week End in Santa Barbara

A girl smiles Eden; the wind blows Arabia;
The sound of a bell touches dark blue on the far wave;
The sky blues away into earth; the earth bends.

Time flutters by, an hour, a day,
(Even a week is a light thing).
But long time is solid,
Long time is heavy, a club to be hit with.

Magnolia, Arkansas-
Los Prietos, California
Spring-Summer 1942

Stranger

I looked for the town.
The leaves were still;
The waves washed under the quay.

I heard tomorrow
And felt today
And the weary wind over the sea.

Strangers walked;
My hat felt alone;
Everyone stood;
No one was to blame.

And only the wind ever said my name.
And the town I found to be stone.

Los Prietos, California
June 8, 1942

"Time fills the canyon . . ."

Time fills the canyon, stillness of dim bowl.
The pine trees grow and stand in it, more still
than stillness, done moving, dreamed in amber time,
called silent, told quiet, cried wilderness by some dead god.

Off, down, free of earth, flown
from arms of trees that hold from the cliff rim, tomorrow lies.

One gray bird goes far below across time—
a simple bird in sunlight,
loose, alive in air below my stand on cliff.

I gaze on time, and oh follow the live bird on its short flight.

Los Prietos, California
June 17, 1942

Los Prietos [I]

Dear friends, the swarthy earth shoulders into the stars here.
The slopes are possessed of many trees.
The gracious sun visits daily the open parks,
and a chaperone mountain serves all the canyon west.
Deer timid through shadows. Birds fly across from cliffs.
Mostly silence rises and moves up the slopes
      past enchanted white spikes of yucca.
This is the land we are exiled to from a world fighting.
We look at each other and sing all the songs we have heard.

Los Prietos, California
June 20, 1942

The Country of Thin Mountains

I tell you, friends, the mountains here are thin—
no more than cardboard propped up there.
And, "What's the difference?" That's what people say.
"We see them; well, what if the far slopes are just painted on?"

And here they have some music made by dying birds.
The sounds are beautiful, I guess,
but back of sound the dying birds, you know . . . .

They like each other here on purpose—to sell things;
and they make love not for forever.

I asked them of their youth, of their dreams,
of old times and places.
They laughed.

I asked about their friends. They said:
"We have no friends. Why should we?
We know our customers?"

And that is how they are.
One thing—they have one mountain that's real.
They do not know it.
They think it's cardboard.

Los Prietos, California
July 1942

Dark-Browed Rough Pacifist

In these rooms where light curtains blow
    and the shining ones are
I listen and tap gongs in the dark-browed
    kennel of my self.
Fast, heavy, and rough are the words, the catches
    of my steps—thinking or walking.
And I watch the shattered glass myself aghast
    after I try.

In the finding of beautiful white flocks among
    other searchers, I wait;
for it's true I have the darker veil across the
    thought and surge toward and over flowers
(the dark sea gulping at the shore flowers,
the jag of pine among the rounded aspens,
the rock breaking the molten stream,
the shadow of a hawk jolting across summer noon).

In these rooms, others quietly speaking
    over deep water, I wait listening.
A bug with mandibles hunts lost in a creation
    of chairs and feet.
Do you know I hear a puppy whimpering?
Do you know I hear the uneasy roll of the
    sagging wind over the house?
Dark-browed rough pacifist, I sit and tap gongs
    in the dark-browed kennel of my self
in these rooms where the shining ones are
    and the light curtains blow.

Los Prietos, California
August 1942

Director

Come down, branch, along the window. There.
The hills now, there. Noon-minted fields
Along the slant beyond. Now still.
This is a place. The salt I taste, this place.
The ruffled storm of seeing this now dies.
In quietness of past the branch comes down—
No good. The world cannot be built and held.
It changes more than we, who taste and go.
The world is not our own, I say it now.
Relaxed the hand, what falls let fall. Hello.
      Goodbye.

> *Los Prietos, California*
> *August 1942*

Discovery [II]

This land, the coast I found, the low dark line
Far-sailing mariners have dreamed in seas,
Lay waiting there, a town hushed in by pine
Sprayed at that sky beyond the leaping trees.
And, rounding hills, the sun, like ours, shone down
As if the place I found was any town.

But here the careful eye could watch the land,
Unmoved, unhurt. All grew out from inside.
No chance thing marred. The spirit reached out wide.
No manifest of stars, no violent hand,

Within the hall where dwelt the careful one
Could brighten or put out that inward sun.

Los Prietos, California
August 1942

Los Prietos [II]

Doves in the dust of our pacifist camp—
and the sky and the deer and the quail
and the wind in the weeds and a baby bat lost
and the darkening west—and here with love is our jail.

There are things to be done, and words said,
and others—but we never have time;
and some we never could say,
so we follow new paths and seek out new names
and hope we can find out a way:
Wrong and Right and Oh Truth!
and Heavy and Light and Dark and then Bright—
and a valley beyond somewhere in the night
and Christ and be good and no harm.

So yes, here we live now like suddenly grass,
beautifully, endlessly frail,
or rocks and old iron—and so don't worry about me:—
always in love with our jail.

Los Prietos, California
August 1942

The Way Men Walk

falling forward,
turning the small delicate bones of the foot from the rocks,
putting the feet in sandals
leathered in and smiled on by falling-forward clerks,
walking out of the sun, under the trees,
bending the arm at last and turning,
putting the feet on the dead leaves and laughing,
and walking away.

Los Prietos, California
August 1942

Night Sound

An acorn falls on our roof in the night
Pattering down to the eaves;
We think our way through the quietness
To the steadfast moon on the leaves.

There in the soul grows a little star,
The heart finds a path to follow;
There in the still is a brimmed-up place,
An arrow of sky, and a swallow.

And over the hill is an always stream
And over the river, trees;
Seeking the hand is another hand,
And the blind have an eye that sees.

Los Prietos, California
September 1942

Rebels

When we look up from sorrow toward the dark,
We know how more than song our singing means.
Our lives from shadows roam a wilderness,
Like stories through silence, hastening
Along the deep dark rocks below a dream
Unheeded by pale women and pale men.
They do not know our kind nor hear our song.
They scorn the dirty splendor they walk on.

Los Prietos, California
October 17, 1942

Breath

Far up the canyon where the salmon leap
and splintered sunlight nails the forest floor
the people without houses put their feet.

And often here below we drag a breath
of something from the wind we missed, and steeply
think: The place we built to live is too near death.

Los Prietos, California
November 1942

Incident

I lived an instant, leaning at rest,
When a candle flame was the most important thing in the world,
When, driven like wind-blown herons over the roof,
Shrilly, shrilly, cold came—white, groping snow,
Came the silentest hungriest wanderers,
Finding below, along roads, among trees,
The silentest ash-fallen creeping things, more aimless than smoke,
And the small furred creatures walking alone in the chaparral.
The snow was a torrent hawk, skimming earth with moveless wings.
And I was that torrent forgetting earth, on relentless, remembering
    wings.

Los Prietos, California
November 1942

Snow

Silently down from Big Pine Mountains, white
Along air paths wind-ordered free and wild
With loneliness to whimper like a child
And messages on rocks and hills to write
Cold justice, on old trees, and then, more mild,
To whisper, drifting promises all night—
Silently down from Big Pine Mountains, white.

Los Prietos, California
November 1942

CO's Work on Mountain Road

Like bay trees on the edge of La Cumbre Peak,
liking with wistful scent the swooping world below,
      we few dreamers
on the edge of new savage years, jagged beyond sight,
audaciously lean, suspiring a few old messages from
      the old earth still under our trustful feet.
The pines have left us and are marching;
the sycamores fly angry tints;
the oaks present overworked postures, extreme.
Who cares in a big country for a few egret trees,
      on one cliff, on an edge, leaning far out,
      on a scent like a memory?

Los Prietos, California
December 23, 1942

Far Down, a River

I held the little trees away,
and looked at the weight
of Santa Cruz Creek
bending in its canyon around Little Pine Mountain.
Held up and slacked by the ridge,
slow through the haze into the sky
went the coast range,
draining space.
And I thought of that river: victim of troubles,

leaning its weight to one cliff and another
—all of them losing to time—
and the helpless course of that river
into the vast triumph and quietness of the sea.

Los Prietos, California
January 15, 1943

"*They say sound is the ear . . .*"

They say sound is the ear and sight the eye
That time is the blood
Scoring a faint blue line over the temple bone.
And it is true that
Blue veins are worn on temples this year
(Teeth are parted: the lips are smiles),

And I believe
There is no land as far as this year's eyes look toward
Or as far as we listen in silence.
The thought that there is such a land is false.

I have not found that land.

Los Prietos, California
February 11, 1943

Search

I went in every house and every room.
I climbed the stairs, descended the basement steps,
   and followed the narrow halls;
And my feet picked up more dust.
And I often stopped, rich with thought.
And when I came to the doors again,
I knew each house.
But it was not home.

Los Prietos, California
February 18, 1943

Meditation

If I could remember all at once—but I have forgotten.
Still, some day, looking along a furrowed cliff, staring
Beyond the eyes' strength, I'll start the avalanche,
And every stone will fall separate and revealed . . . .

Los Prietos, California
March 1943

Tragedy

In a big plank room in the mountains
A bunch of men
Listened to a man
Talk about tragedy.

As he spoke I realized
The skulls of the starving
The great dark eyes
The death in humanity,
The amorphous unhuman suffering.

A wave of silence was over that room
In the mountains.
And the speaker, I knew, couldn't know,
With the eloquence,
Without wilting.

He would have [been] lost in the drift of thought.
He would have trembled before us all.
He would have knelt on the old plank floor,
And could not have spoken.

Los Prietos, California
March 1943

Walking at Night

Now I am alone, following the downwar slur
Of blowing sleet past lights, and I remember:
The tremendous little train, quiet now with evening,
Sagging along that valley on the way home;
Those fragile Sunday mornings,
The men and women giving those days away,
Never caring what comes over the curve of the earth,
Measuring juke box life by drinks in a war boom bar,
Wearing wings from death by terror across the ocean;
Those walls sweeping together with walls in corners of knot-eyed wood;
Those persons looking at each other, their lives a richness;
And transported choirs of heroes on a buoyant sea.

Now, in time of darkness and cold,
Those islands of fairness, piercing and staggering,
Live breathlessly like children dashing through a room;
And I have become a student of having
And not having.

Los Prietos, California
March 1943

"We called it the chaparral . . ."

We called it the chaparral,
folded, easily draped and softly a comfort
over that land egg-beatered out of rock.
It lapped over our cliff

and rested like an evening of shade above
     the breaks of the river;
a soft statement of greenness, down all
     the hills,
in wide forgiveness, a layer of dew and night
     that never moves on:

the dimension of life on that land.

Called chaparral:
in the night a deepness all over our land,
containing the sleeping birds and the
     quiet deer,
reaching soft fingers of distance,
becoming a lawn on mountain shoulders
or a shagginess on the near slope;

gazed at by eagles and men.

The shaggy old pelt of our land,
worried by rain and by sun,
a shawl over Little Pine Mountain,
a pelt over Cachuma Ridge,
a help and a quietness as high as our heads
as we walked with pilgrim souls
     toward the rocky hills,
those permanent gestures,
inland or toward the sea.

Los Prietos, California
March 1943

Here, Now

One step after another across and over the land.
(How far away was that first step that led to where I stand!)

One hill, then a hill, then another, over and over again.
(Lost past a thousand ridges is a valley hidden in rain.)

Rainbows arching forever, beyond vaulting over the hill.
(The sun on that roof and the song are gone, and the people, still.)

I stand here among boulders in a place where flowers don't care.
(How the sun shone deep above our town on its tower of golden air!)

Los Prietos, California
April 1943

Apology

There was a flowering bush one time by where I walked:
I didn't stop; I was in a hurry.
One time someone was talking: and I didn't listen.
I stayed up one night late, watching:
but I went to sleep before morning.
My hands were shaking one time in class.
My coat was too long in the sleeves.
Now I feel that I am a prisoner here.
My old coat speaks for me,
The curtness of my words, my angry eyes—
these imply a jailer somewhere—everyone's jailer.

Long ago a man picked me up when I fell:
I did not look him long enough in the eye.

Have you seen that man?

Where does our jailer live?
What are the terms we are on?
Why?

Los Prietos, California
May 13, 1943

Prison Camp

I heard the homeless laugh.
I heard the prisoner sing.
I knew I could not leave my place with them for anything.

Across the yard and the grass
I saw those men and their friends go—
helpless, proud, deaf and blind with youth like snow:—

Their lives a slanting toward earth,
their passing a soft blur on the eye;
white, white in the heart, and on the hills
that snowflake, songflake, thoughtflake went by.

Los Prietos, California
June 1943

"While we sat on the lawn ..."

While we sat on the lawn in the shade,
pursuing with talk our task—food, help,
reconstruction all over the world—
I looked across the fields and at the loop of green
foliage along the river in the sun;
and there, coming up in a swelling wave,
trampling the rank pasture from the south,
the hot afternoon wind laid its whole looseness
against those far-off shimmering trees,
turning up the branches and silvering the leaves.
And I thought of all the times I've seen that—
noons in the Kansas wheat, trips along the river,
lying at rest after a fire in the mountains of California,
standing with Tom and Dan waiting for a ride,
at San Marcos Pass, there by the live oaks, wonderfully made,
    and a valley . . .
The wind against the silvered leaves,
        the world turning round.

                                 Manchester College, Indiana
                                 July 5, 1943

"I was there when it happened ..."

I was there when it happened—
the singing over the hill,
and sound in the air like a sliding wind
and a movement of bush, then still.

I was there when it happened—
I saw the dead go by,
the scorn of earth on their ghostly shoes,
the open stare of the sky.

I was there when it happened—
nothing moved; I was there.
On other fields there was killing,
and the wind was combing my hair.

I don't know what I'd do, he said,
if they hadn't sung in that dream.
I think I'd regret the world, he said,
if things were the way they seem.

I am a man with hope and eyes,
yes, hope, and hurt, and a prayer,
and I am awake when the dim thoughts come,
when it happens I am there.

Los Prietos, California
August 7, 1943

Family Statement

My brother, flying a plane in this war,
    may come up that long ramp to the exit
    and go into tomorrow.
He may turn his face away from our small play
    by the mulberry tree, and kill a man.
(These days, I put my hand on the stone wall at the corner,

turning and looking back:
I wear the old hat, and the tie he sent.)

My brother is in the army that wins, swearing, proud of a flag,
    made happy by movies.
The common soldier is hero in this war:
    my brother was there, in the crowd,
    when a hero, in a ceremony on a stage, kissed Tana Randis
(currently seen in *Land of Desire*).
(Every morning my feet hurry these leaves under these trees.
I won't walk another street till this one is worn out by the sun.)

My brother, in the army that wins, and I
    remember those times when Pop came home
    and everyone meeting him at the door.
My brother and I are both crying
    in this glittering chromium time
    in the saddest war.

Los Prietos, California
August 11, 1943

Current

All braided into torrents falls
what enters that dark tunnel toward the sea—
I wonder how far off the stillness calls
from which the swirling lost flows on past me?

Below the sun, in eyes, along these halls,
I watch the living flow on secretly—
I wonder how far off the stillness calls
from which the swirling lost flows on past me?

Los Prietos, California
August 15, 1943

Like Whitman

If any time was used preparing
No preparing is wasted.
No preparing at all is wasted.
I am meeting you wherever you are.
I am on my way.
Do not let the distance and the time
    of that way influence you.
I am coming toward you.
Do you know anything of the breakers?
    (Whatever the wind, the rocks, the wilderness)
Do you know those cold barriers of the world and of people?
    (Whatever holds back, outside and inside)
Do you realize no preparation is ever wasted?
    (I am coming toward you).

Los Prietos, California
August 27, 1943

Easy

Our men walk lightly and scatter over the mountains.
They go away casually and you can't find them.
You can't ever find them. They don't care.
They don't even tie their shoes or look back.
They climb over the rocks and stand easily in the sun.
They can build roads and lift stones all day and laugh on the way home.

You ask them a question, but you can't ever find them.
"God don't like war," says one.
"I'll go back, I'm willing. I'll walk the rows of corn," says another.
"But why should I kill people? It's silly."
They stroll through those tall mountains.
They don't care.

Los Prietos, California
September 15, 1943

Nocturne [I]

Gone, gone. So silent.
Footfall. Leaf off the bough.
Laughter yesterday, faded.
These are the times, now.

Warm, warm. Turning the world down,
Touch like the warm rain,
Flowers forever,
Rain on the green soft plain.

Reaching a hand,
Twirling the dial,
We tune in the world again,
On trial.

Los Prietos, California
October 22, 1943

"spoke about sacrifice . . ."

spoke about sacrifice
and valor
(that's when the drum
spoke about Jesus)

sailed here across the sea
and landed
(heard the whole world
speaking with cannon)

saw men in uniform
and killed them
(I think that the drum
spoke about Jesus)

Los Prietos, California
November 7, 1943

"Your tragedy before the ship goes down . . ."

Your tragedy before the ship goes down,
Your tragedy before the engines die,
Is here: They lived, and came from any town;
Some one ran after them, and said goodbye.

Los Prietos, California
December 21, 1943

"I do not know how that fine dust rises . . ."

I do not know how that fine dust rises in the South and follows the
    slow breathing air—
Buoyant, one flake at a time, and resistless comes down everywhere
At night on philosophers and movie stars,

But whatever the deepening change in the wars,
Erosion of faces and faith all over the world,
We know that deepening change, that fate—dust on the breakfast plate.

Los Prietos, California
December 31, 1943

More Than Bread

I do not want to live here.
The water is good, and the soil grows corn.
The people like each other.

I do not want to live here.
The land slopes right,
   and the sun likes it here.
There is incredible white snow in the winter.

But every day a native of the world falls down.
Many are hurt in the mills and in the fields.
Some day everyone will be blind.

I do not want to just live here.

Los Prietos, California
January 19, 1944

"Shall we have that singing . . ."

Shall we have that singing in the evening?
For between the stars and our star there is no one.
And we must sleep again.
We rest the hands, not dangerous, on the wool.
And we place pillows under the turning head.

Quietly now, no moving,
Was there something forgotten?

(The losing one neglects and calls it winning.)
Help each other.
Have that singing in the evening.

Los Prietos, California
January 19, 1944

These Mornings

Watch our smoke curdle up out of the chimney
    into the canyon channel of air.
The wind shakes it free over the trees
    and hurries it into nothing.

Today there is more smoke in the world
    than ever before.
There are more cities going into the sky,
    helplessly, than ever before.

The cities today are going away into the sky,
    and what is left is going into the earth.

This is what happens when a city is bombed:
    Part of that city goes away into the sky,
    And part of that city goes into the earth.
And that is what happens to the people when a city is bombed:
    Part of them goes away into the sky,
    And part of them goes into the earth.
And what is left, for us, between the sky and the earth
    is a scar.

Los Prietos, California
January 20, 1944

Speech from a Play

The reason you cannot say anything is you were not there.
No one knows. No one was there. . . .

I heard his voice while they were taking him away.
And after he was gone, I could remember it.
The people around me now will never hear it.
There is nothing anyone can do against the voice.
It is the person with you in a room. All with you.
No one knows how much.
Arrest me—I hear it now. . . .

Los Prietos, California
January 21, 1944

Nocturne [II]

I will call you by your softest name.
Though snow will fall along the farthest hill,
Winter will end; nothing will be the same.
At first we will not know; and then we will.

Down all the long unceasing height of day,
Into our eyes and gently on the land,
The snow will say its whiteness, and I'll say
Your softest name, your hand within my hand.

Los Prietos, California
January 22, 1944

Christmas Comes but Once a Year

What they told us on Christmas was all right.
They put the town on like an old coat and wore it.
That was all right.
They said hello, and poor people walked by.
They gave awards to leading citizens,
    who took those awards.
Everyone said: Honesty is the best policy.
    It pays to advertise.
    The best defense is a good offense.
That was all right—
    just so it snowed on Christmas.

They went to the movies of Austria and Poland and France,
    and the Negroes sat in the balcony.
That was all right—
    just so the family could be together on Sunday.

There were bright fast cars and beggars on the streets.
Factories sold things in countries never heard of.
    (The marines knew of those countries.)
That was all right.
The children fought the whole world—
    and won only when they grew up, coming into their own.
That was all right—
    just so the kids were cute and innocent.

The old were everywhere, selling papers.
And some were tired, while others played.
That was all right.

Some one would manage.
It was all all right—
　　just so it snowed on Christmas.

Los Prietos, California
February 13, 1944

Immediate

If there is anyone
　　between our star and other stars
If there is anyone
　　what heaven he sees is here with us.

　　　　Between our words
　　　　before our feet
　　　　coming towards
　　　　us down our street.

If there is any light
　　I think it lies
unasked for by our hands,
　　behind our eyes.

　　　　Between our words
　　　　before our feet
　　　　coming towards
　　　　us down our street.

If there is any word
  we softly wait
The farthest answer comes
  within our gate.

      Between our words
      before our feet
      coming towards
      us down our street.

Los Prietos, California
February 14, 1944

War Guilt

The pupil of the sun
The iris of the sky
The one great stare of day
Is on what we have done
And what we say.

We did not want a gun
We did not want to die
Yet we have killed a man, they say
Each one:
Look down, sky.

The gazing sun goes out
The lid of day
Goes down with doubt:
What war is won
Today?

We all have done
Our work. We sing:
"I have not killed a man
—not one, today—
for anything."

Los Prietos, California
March 9, 1944

Fate

More steadfast than a truck
Along a narrow street
A minute looks for you
Until you meet.

Los Prietos, California
March 13, 1944

Devotion

Along my river frogs like thought
plop into depths before my foot.

Lift of the wind will drop a crumb—
a fragment of my gleaming home.

Put on like shoes, my face will have
delight, for each day's epitaph.

And I will raise my head and care:
Oh orphan world, I love you dear.

Los Prietos, California
March 21, 1944

To a Gold Star Mother

Which are the men who killed your son?
    We all, praising the deed he's done.
Where is the fate that made him die?
    We, liking splendor marching by.
Who make war that stills his heart?
    We, loving your son—we make wars start.

Los Prietos, California
March 23, 1944

At a Little Church

Following the velvet trail, I found their shrine.
In song and moving they were kind and grave.
Whatever they could give, they called it mine,
And all that mortals could give, they gave.

I followed where they went and marked their words;
I knelt down by their fires and heard their tale.
I watched their children play—they flit like birds.
And in the night, their weak—I saw them fail.

I tried to touch their hands, to tell some way
How brave they are and noble, standing there;
But how could that be spoken? Could I say
Their sadness and their joy? How much I care?

I learned the way they stand and how they sing:—
All that I have. They gave me everything.

Los Prietos, California
March 25, 1944

"You might as well put . . ."

You might as well put
your hand on stone
and look at the banner maples.

You might as well pack
your old black trunk
and fasten it down with staples.

You might as well go
by Clement's bridge
and climb away tonight.

You might as well like
a soldier's life
'cause you're going to have to fight.

Whatever is left
will be done by air
or put on a government bill.

If you liked it here
why you can look back
tonight, climbing the hill.

Los Prietos, California
March 31, 1944

"The One who said 'No violence'..."

The One who said "No violence"
Said "mountains,"
And they are here, storm-violent, of stone.
Whoever looks across their peaks and wonders
Will feel that friendly men are all alone.
That all alone they speak to one another,
That all alone they build or they repair.
They stand and look, unmoved, beyond the mountains,
"There surely lie rich plains," they say,
"Out there."

Fredonyer Pass, California
May 21, 1944

Counsel

If any ask, say yes.
    It is all true.

If any try, encourage them.
    They'll do.

If any blame, bow low.
    They will be right.

If any fear, sit down by them
    and stare at night.

Fredonyer Pass, California
May 24, 1944

Fire in Lava Country

Part of the earth not made to walk on
Has bloomed in flame, and we are sent
To walk in every place and stop that fire,
And we go through black woods the way fire went.

So much of every world is dead and cracked
We have to save that part to save the rest.
We spend the night at work improving bad,
And wait for dawn to build homes on the best.

Fredonyer Pass, California
May 28, 1944

"It's an old story . . ."

It's an old story,
it's like this—

You spend a day and you have it.
You feel there is a storm waiting
    above every storm,
And a silent heart
    in every heart,
And your way is a river, deepening;
And each night has many undelivered stars.
You become a listener;
You can't lose what you give away;
And you live each day for keeps.

Fredonyer Pass, California
May 29, 1944

We Kindred

Whoever stands uncertain in the night
And sees porch, steps, and boards along the floor,
And hears a train go tearing in wild flight
Along the edge of dark he listens for
May have my home and possess all my land.

For he has known (plain coat, plain face, plain eyes)
A kingdom in the dark, where heroes stand

And watch a place each watcher owned go by
Before a bubble breaks at some night sound
And wrecks that place the resting heart had found.

Fredonyer Pass, California
June 7, 1944

Home

Our father owned a star,
and by its light
we lived in father's house
and slept at night.

The tragedies of life,
like death and war,
were faces looking in
at our front door.

But finally all came in,
from near and far:
you can't believe in locks
and own a star.

Peg Leg Lookout, California
June 21, 1944

Little Sermon

The butterfly, the bee, the hummingbird
do business with color and are wise.
They wear their wings on earth for Paradise.

The brightest of the prophets of the Word:
the butterfly, the bee, the hummingbird.

Gansner Bar, California
August 16, 1944

Isaiah, '44

The people who tried to walk
    on the watered stock
have drowned in the world.

They have gone down in some cave
    under the lava.
They sank past the news-stands
    and the lecturers;
and past the friends who
    wondered a little now and then;
and they let the straw clerks in the store go by
    without clutching them.

The people who turned electric fans
    on the salt of their brow
have fallen down.

They suffered the little children
     to work for them.
They built a big needle's eye
     made out of churches;
and there the acrobatic camels knelt down.
(They can go six days without milk,
     but on the seventh, they drown.)

They walked past the big red sign,
     and the last corner where the singing was.
They got in the big cars and said "Home."
     And were drowned.

Gansner Bar, California
September 16, 1944

"They taught me to be hurt . . ."

They taught me to be hurt.
I don't know why.
They held my hand till dark,
Then said goodbye.

And those who held me up
Grew weaker then.
And those I thought were gods
Were frightened men.

Such gods, who told me wise
And left me dumb,
Will have to call me long
Before I'll come.

Fredonyer Pass, California
September 18, 1944

A Posy

Some people keep
    a large and savage messiah
    chained in the front yard.
They drive around on
    retread platitudes.
Their scripture is in
    a steelbacked Bible.
They go to the circus
    in the evening edition
    to see the Christians
    lose to the lions again.

Fredonyer Pass, California
September 20, 1944

"They flawed when struck . . ."

They flawed when struck,
But no one knew their flaw.
They faltered just that once,
But no one saw.

And no one helped.
The people hurried on.
And no one knew the hurt
And what was gone.

Till time took youth
Away—and that was when
Their sky came tumbling down:
They shattered then.

Fredonyer Pass, California
September 21, [1944]

Listening

Our wilderness the world
Is growing in the rain.
Learning help from friends
And being less alone.

Out of silent land
A rising music moves
And comes to all who wait
Like night wind over groves.

Every little tree
Calls out from its own coomb,
And the roots of cedars creep
Lost in the forest mold.

But in that forest sleeps
A man who one day hears,
And shakes an answer out
Like streamers over stars.

Big Springs, Old Station, California
October 1, 1944

Speech from the Big Play

—the height over the cabin—

Not many of you in the world remember
    that old scene in the cabin at night
    when the guttering flame made shadows eager
    along the wall.

Not many, I am afraid, remember
    the homely stanchions of our kind back then,
    and the taste of the days like cider—
    rife, cool, and wild,
    along the roads we stooped to build
    or to carry things along.

But now and then we turn on the sound of the world
    and listen, as we did one night,
    there in the tents in Little Bunch Grass Valley.

We turned on the fever of history,
    and the pulse headache of flicker-ad cities,
    here and gone tomorrow on the wrinkled earth.

And from there we saw how—
    the slope where people lived,
    down along the shallower streams,
    missed big storms in the fall.
People forgot winter—the cold fastening
    on branches, bark, stone;
    and the gentler stone of lynx, marten,
    and squirrel.
They knew not the drifting of snow—
    the forgetting of edges, and points, and ruts;
    and the looming of gauntness into Thanksgiving.
But they learned about one snowflake at a time;
    forever they studied the rules of winter,
    after the homecoming avalanche.
Then all dwellers preferred to share winter
    a little at a time, with lynx, marten,
    and squirrel,
    before forgotten in the steeper land,
    where the burden fell on those in the cold
    and finally slid to rest on the sheltered ones.

And we saw how—

Steady, crowding the needles, sighing,
    pulling the limbs like taffy,
    a wind out of the wide valley
    broke smoothly away, and carried
    in one breath the small breaths.

And we saw—

Beyond the flow of trees
   the flow of hills.
And then the flow of sky,
   smooth-resting on the dome.
And, walking near the willows,
   flowing men—
Slow, positive, in heavy boots;
   then gone past the gauzy limbs
   bent finally down.

And then we knew—

The shadows of people are Lincoln.
With malice toward none coming onto the back porch,
hanging up the coat, scraping the boots.
The moon over the fields is Illinois,
   in winter, before 1900.
The lines of tall houses in the country
   are the correct, upright, upward destiny
   of before the war.

We hear the crash of ice on rivers, the breaking
   of dams, the sirens of ambulances
   in the city.
But everyone has a shadow like Lincoln,
   frailty made rugged and kindly
   including us all.

Belden, California
November 1944

One Place I Saw

In that bright place the earth is always dry
Long afternoons.
The thunder-beaten mountains tower high
Like amber dunes.
One time I lived there. Wind in grooves blew down
The carven scarp
Of cedar slopes; and shaking aspens made the town
A windmill harp.
I felt the mountains, sky, the whole earth pinned.
I went away.
Where time lay deep below the carving wind
I couldn't stay.

Belden, California
January 1, 1945

Before the Big Storm

You are famous in my mind.
When anyone mentions your name
all the boxes marked "1930s"
fall off the shelves;
and the orators on the Fourth of July
all begin shouting again.
The audience of our high school commencement
begin to look out of the windows at the big storm.

And I think of you in our play—
oh, helpless and lonely!—crying,
and your father is dead again.
He was drunk; he fell.

When they mention your name,
our houses out there in the wind
creak again in the storm;
and I lean from our play, wherever I am,
to you, quiet at the edge of that town:
"All the world is blowing away."
"It is almost daylight."
"Are you warm?"

Belden, California
January 3, 1945

"Unto a great a great deaf mountain . . ."

Unto a great deaf mountain
I made a sign,
Claiming one valley of silence
Mine.

Men call the farthest valley—
Everything—theirs.
They think the great deaf mountain
Hears!

Belden, California
January 5, 1945

The Tall Animals

For pigs the click of the pail is enough.
They stumble and crowd and run,
heads down, without thought, and wait,
ugly and gruff,
by the gate
for a crumb,
from you or from anyone.
Even for garbage they come.

But the way the tall animals come is this way.
They follow the line of the trees.
They turn from the hillside and look.
They stand by the stream.
If they know you and like you they come.
They nuzzle your hand
and then stand,
as much as to say:
We test everything. Since we like you, we stay.

Gansner Bar, California
January 28, 1945

Footnote

When they captured Ishi, the last wild Indian, near Oroville,
the stone age ended like the end of a film.
He thought the handcuffs a bright steel gift.
He didn't know anything worth knowing.

They gave him three cigars a day
and a job in a museum.

Gansner Bar, California
February 2, 1945

Travel Report: 1945

Saying "King's X," a man might walk,
Standing tall and not looking down,
Along the Rhine and through Norway
And all those countries mowed with steel;
And he could bestow with half-closed eyes,
A leafy restoration.

But he would have to look far, and be slow,
Travel mostly by dusk on old roads,
And often to say "King's X" if his eyes grew wide.

Gansner Bar, California
February 2, 1945

All White

Without a door closing
without one candle of light
tremendously, we found,
snow fell. All white.

It fell on thick cedars bowed
miles deep from the liberal cloud
weighing a mile to a pound,
tremendously without sound

That night.

Belden, California
February 13, 1945

Chicago Bridge, Evening

Listen, you whistles and gongs;
    listen, you clanging mouth,
What can you say when hope's away
    and spring has gone down South.
Spring has died down South.

Listen, smoke over the town;
    listen with your big ears.
Lightning for wit, you idiot,
    but never a word for tears.
Never a help for tears.

Elgin, Illinois
March 2, 1945

"That land spoke . . ."

That land spoke.
It spoke all day.
It cried out at sunset.
I never have held out my hands to a fire like its fire.
And I never have turned my head in any cap
      toward more granite a talker,
      more serious a word.
The word lay out there before us,
      uttered in desolation.
Let us never go back without a bigger heart:
The place I went under was there,
      at Socorro.

Elgin, Illinois
March 9, 1945

Listener

Like a big black dog I followed your question home.
It lived in a house on a crooked narrow street.
Do not twist my hat in your eyes, or in your reaching palm;
I don't live anymore in that little stone under your feet.

I followed your look; I followed those things you said.
The trail led North into a land like a star.
I won't be back from the tundra beyond your word.
Like a big black dog I followed the trail too far.

Elgin, Illinois
March 11, 1945

Flickerings

I'm glad the heart sleeps.
It might wake, splitting night
    with hurt like a thunderstorm.
Or raise the far edge of black
    and lower like dawn.
I'm glad the heart sleeps.

It might stir, and grow white.
It might.
It might never get warm,
wake, listen, lonely, in rain.
Might never lie easy again.
I'm glad the heart sleeps.

Elgin, Illinois
March 15, 1945

"I had forgotten the clown . . ."

I had forgotten the clown in me
    and the tragedian.
I couldn't read my lines without the fustian—
I was about to lose the homestead or win the fair lady:
I could never speak just flat and go on with the business.
All my dramas were hundreds of little, simultaneous dramas.
Couldn't I ever leave that act about my
    rabbit that died and gave up when Jane's lived?
Or my dog that wouldn't be mine and was killed?
Some day I want to go on stage one man,

and hear the plot and say one short clean say.
Now, as it is, I have to walk on a wide
      long bridge and see the gulls and the crinkled wind,
I have to do some thing like that carefully
if ever I want to leave the depths of me
and the unsolved plays below my play.

[Elgin, Illinois]
March 15, 1945

The War Season

The birds that winter blew past our yard
      feathered along so young
that only the trees could follow their wings
      or understand their tongue.

The north wind blew. Limbs bent down.
      Leaves fell over the lawn.
The birds one day were young in the sky;
      the next day they were gone.

Elgin, Illinois
April 18, 1945

Translation from the Yaqui

The hairy-faced who walk like aged bears
Climb into canyons—none too low or high;
They trade their horses for dull yellow stone:
What white men buy!

The fathers at the mission ring old bells;
They live to lift bad men who ought to die;
Their Jesus paid to save such rogues from Hell:
What white men buy!

Elgin, Illinois
May 7, 1945

Twelve Years Old

Tired that day we were; we found
honey in an old tree.
Small we were, tired and small.
No one remembers but me:—

Honey there in the broken branch,
honey found in the wild;
you looking out over bending grass,
and looking far, for a child—

Far to a land all curved and green,
a place the wind blew from,
a poured-out land all honey smooth—
a land that never did come.

Elgin, Illinois
May 15, 1945

The Midgets of War

The midgets of war have loud hollow guns
That make a tremendous roar,
But the giants of growth aim trees at the sun
And build homes for the midgets of war.

Fredonyer Pass, California
May 24, 1945

Mr. Conscience

The meditative crane
with angular zigzag brain
thinks:

What kind of world am I wading in?

Wait.
Stalk fish:

Where does the me begin?

Step.
Flash the thin thinker,
swish,
to kill.

Wades on.
The answer in his bill.

Elgin, Illinois
June 6, 1945

Nine-Year's Dream

You have made tracks in our snow!
You have broken deep silence at night!
A giant God watches, you know.
. . . Only so little; just nine years old.

You killed the bird on the limb!
You thought your mother as dead!
You thought of your father—yes, what of him?
. . . Only so little; just nine years old.

You laughed when the dead child fell!
You hid in the shadow and saw!
You knew the desperate and never would tell!
. . . Only so little; just nine years old.

Elgin, Illinois
June 21, 1945

"The first thing that grows . . ."

The first thing that grows in the spring,
before the fern,
is tragedy.
Growing in the gray rain
from the eyes looking out
and then closed from a window.

The stars fell down in the night
in the spring.
And inside you stand and hear the sound
of the tragedies growing
in the rain in the woods around you.

Elgin, Illinois
July 28, 1945

The Sound: Summer, 1945

Not a loud sound, the buzz of the rattlesnake.
But urgent. Making the heart pound a loud drum.
Somewhere in dead weeds by a dry lake
On cracked earth flat in the sun.

The living thing left raises the fanged head,
Tormented and nagged by the drouth,
And stares past a planet that's dead,
With anger and death in its mouth.

Elgin, Illinois
August 8, 1945

Victory

All violent like the knife that drove
the pity-begging life out through the eyes,
and wilted the choked voice in little cries
    that bubbled and blinked out along the floor.

All hungry like the outlaw stare that tore
the North and reeled the rivers in along the spool
that never would unwind them anymore
    to wander cool
but stretched them taut to all that's far away.

All lost by dusty roads, all fled with love,
all hid along with play:
all hurt by what we lost who conquered in the war—
    so violent, so lost, so far away.

Elgin, Illinois
August 16, 1945

"A note on solemn war . . ."

A note on solemn war:
    the charnel stench of all medals
    the tide of tears through every marching song
    the black scream blotted over the heads of orators
    behind the scenes, the sound of creaking, higher into hysteria
    the cold implacable murder in national anthems
    the strait-jacket badge of cruel insanity in uniforms

the ferreting out and rewarding of childish aggression, bullying
    vainglory, relentless hate
A note on solemn war:
    the charnel stench of all medals.

Elgin, Illinois
August 17, 1945

On Attending a Militaristic Church Service

And there I sat on my swami
holding my nose in the pews,
under the nozzle of preaching
to be washed in the blood of the news.

Elgin, Illinois
September 8, 1945

Nine Years Old

Violence lowered its lids of silence;
with priority, hate was sedate—
    it brought worth,
    respect,
    and in all the rooms first place:
And Right was in the powerful arms of the
    grownup human race.

Mr. before the name meant something might happen.
And Miss meant something never had.
And Mrs. meant something always did.

And all of our land was permanently occupied
    by an army of grownup Pattons;
and the defeated were the seen and not heard—
    the well-behaved little kids.

Elgin, Illinois
September 24, 1945

CO Week End

When we went into town
Each bore a limb of pine
To hold before his face and sing
Like nobody was crying.

The grass had shined our shoes.
The wind had combed our hair.
To hear of grace we went to church
And begged from door to door.

The climate of the world
Was pools in which we swam,
But eyes of citizens ran ads
With one word: "Uniform."

The navy owned the sea;
The army owned the land;
And we sang through our limb of pine
To hold the time we had.

Elgin, Illinois
October 31, 1945

"Over the candle we looked at us . . ,"

Over the candle we looked at us, each one;
always just talk, never a word to go
under the wall or through the bars to prison.

Solitary men, wardens would never know
how by ourselves we sentenced each other there,
waiting for pardons, waiting each one for his own.

Over the table we looked; no one was fair;
everyone fled. We talked a loud silence, on, without belief,
each one afraid that no one who heard would hear.
Ever, our talking low shouted our grief.
Everyone fled in talk that was easy with fear.

Elgin, Illinois
November 17, 1945

Assay

They found the big mine of honesty
out in the wide valley.
And bright flaked nuggets of truth
swirled in the clear talk of the country folk.

Thousands of prospectors moved in
and sank a deep shaft into the mother lode
and grew rich.
They say that their product and what they mined
was as good as gold.

Elgin, Illinois
December 4, 1945

Review

The arm is bayonet good
and the feet for marching.
The eyes can lick over a blasted town
and then read a menu.
The voice can sing anthems for action
and then pray.

But the heart is not fit enough.
    It can't arm itself.
    It can't march.
    It cannot even beat near a blasted town
    and then sing.

The heart is rejected for military service,
or for essential civilian duty.

What are you doing here, heart?
Heart? whose side are you on?

Elgin, Illinois
December 5, 1945

Note

The sparrows are as reckless as ever.
They don't care whether they fall.
I watch their wings this winter—
vigorous birds, but a crumbling wall.

Elgin, Illinois
December 31, 1945

1946–1947

Return

Home through the flashing lights
    under the white steam plume
    along the great grooved steel
    out of the clanging dark
    stopped at last in the night
    home.

Home with a long winged swoop
    out of the crowded sky
    steep through the hard cruel air
    down with a shuddering gust
    with engine that goes to sleep
    home.

Home not heard to arrive
    quietly step from the boat
    feet like wool in the grass
    boots like down in the snow
    then face alight in the door
    and home,
    alive.

[Elgin, Illinois]
January 4, 1946

"I thought they shouldn't turn the light so low . . ."

I thought they shouldn't turn the light so low
that current trembled in the darkened wire;
and I saw fear in eyes of those who know,
who prayed till night came in the coil on fire.

And then we crept into a great black hall
and heard a loud voice cry "Prepare for war!"
No one said anything; we heard, that's all.
The lights were out, and no one asked what for.

Elgin, Illinois
January 12, 1946

Easy Art

They have preached flowers for so long,
that I lean reeds beside my door.
That's my creed.

They travel to hear music;
I listen to learn what waits to soar
from any word.

Or to stray from the flaring swerve
of a tumbleweed.

[Elgin, Illinois]
January 15, 1946

"They listened to him say his creed . . ."

They listened to him say his creed
and said he was a blackbird singing on a reed.
Have you ever heard a blackbird?—listened to him long?
The room turned so quiet the curtains breathed.
And we who heard the blackbird song believed.

Elgin, Illinois
January 27, 1946

To Those among Us Who Will Be Wise, and Know

When we saw all of our friends, the helpers together,
Walk off alone after the feast in the hall,
We knew each one would probably offend the other.
That is the way men are—forgetting their lasting
Hall, bigger than feasts or time of days.

We are here, you looking down and sorry away.
Always here, and love you, not knowing how,
Even as we too walk on an outward road.

We have moved our whole town up around you.
We are on that bluff and along that shore.
Our gray, steam-breath ponies have dragged the boards
And the nails and shingles up through the snow.
Through the dusk, up through the cold thick flurries,
You can gaze wherever, wherever you are.
All of our doors are open, the fireplace is burning,
We just wait; no one is calling, no one is hurried.

We have surprised you. Where you thought the wolves
And hunger, a shrill wind at night and shaking bare woods,
We have our town—that's where all of us are.

Berkeley, California
March 7, 1946

Deep Listening

The taut wire hums before it breaks,
    like the city in the morning
    or late, when the lights go out.
And the chain on the bridge gate—
    before it snaps, one link turns over
    slowly, and creaks.

I watch an oak whose top
    has forgotten the ground under the leaves.
At the final swing of the axe
    the high branches glisten,
    whisper, then lean
    with surging recognition
    to an old friend.

I turn to you
    and listen.

Berkeley, California
March 12, 1946

"You dropped into my morning..."

You dropped into my morning a sound;
It lay without breaking,
   like a mushroom,
And grew at noon,
   or when touched a cold window
   or hand or word.

And it rose in the evening
   like a balloon through mist
And rolled and shattered to nothing,
   at sleep, on the throat, on the tongue.

And they all rose, every one,
All slow; not one lasted.
The lone walker by lakes
The look over the snow
The place where the trees leaned down
All the wide home.

When I touched them they broke;
While I watched them they all went away.

[Berkeley, California]
March 30, 1946

Campanile

How many young have gone by here slow
Hearing the iron beat what heroes sang?
The books, the long bright halls close ranged,
The very stones crying loud and low
Are trying to tell a little part inside
What leaned over the shoulders of men and cried
And whispered when the heart like a carillon rang.

[Berkeley, California]
April 9, 1946

Two Bits Worth

I heard some oath in boots mug the red beer
They cask in headlines North and South,
And I knew some bloody sots brewed pain
From such grain in a liar's mouth:

Wait—shall we foam the open ear to war again?
Such booted oaths led past a million graves to here.

Berkeley, California
April 11, 1946

"When I walked along the earth . . ."

When I walked along the earth,
many a worthless thing lay
without honor in the shade.

And often the fern brushed my hand
as I went by the track
and often I looked back.

Those worthless things were precious,
and if I come this way again
I will touch like fern each one.

Berkeley, California
May 4, 1946

So Long

Of the millions of rain
one fell on the window
between me and the city,

one fell on your cheek
as I turned to look
when they started the train,

one blurred this letter
down near the end
above my name.

Berkeley, California
May 9, 1946

Human Song

Whenever we loved, our hearts were rolled
Like tinkling glass in the mountains of our world.

We did not know how.
We gathered faggots and laid them on a fire.
We smoothed the rude earth for a bed,
And woke up tired.

When we laid away our mothers and fathers
We swayed our arms and raised a slow song;
Not one thing did we know how to do,
It was all wrong.

Our boots leaked in the cold marshes.
Our children fell and cried on the sharp stones.
Our houses leaned in the autumn storms,
And so did our bones.

We did not know how to call on the stars
Or how to lay our dead in memories of pearl,
Or to follow them far.
They were alone in the earth;
They went there without us
Without the canopy of our love—from birth.

Our life had no texture, no woven strands;
It parted like dry rushes in our hands.

And whenever we loved, our hearts were rolled
Like tinkling glass in the mountains of our world.

Berkeley, California
May 16, 1946

Occurrences

One dead still night our town lay near the wilderness,
And a mountain lion prowled past vacant lots
And curved his head like a ray from fate along the fence
Toward the neighbors' house. Their dog went shrill with warning,
But the neighbor slept.

For three days last winter a river of wind roared
Out of the gray West and over the flattened hills
Around our house till the trees broke and the wall trembled.
On the last day a bird fell limp and ragged at the door.
We buried him in the garden.

I saw down by our lake a tall figure over by the island,
And I called far with care not to frighten and rowed over to
    the place,
But the reeds were waving without any breeze. Many waited
For me and I was late; so I hurried on to my job in town
Where everyone says good morning.

Berkeley, California
May 20, 1946

"All around the biggest bay . . ."

All around the biggest bay the curious hive,
the city, goes;
they are building something there.
What, nobody knows.

Over one hill is the range.
Just weeds and grass; the sage is gray.
In the morning I look at the city,
at night, away.

Berkeley, California
June 2, 1946

Demolition Project

Turn off the rocker where Momma sewed;
click off the birds that hopped:
Momma would cry to see the years rush by
and all of the old life stopped.

Close up the pantry where Momma sang;
think all of the old house down:
sit quietly here and give it a tear;
roll up the old home town.

Berkeley, California
July 21, 1946

Foundations

Some invisible tower
Stands under every star
From every soul on earth
Who gazes up that far.

Traveling, steep and slow,
Out from a mild regard
The tower invisible climbs,
And stands there, silver-starred.

Glendale, California
August 16, 1946

Home Town from the Flyer

The leaves, the stir of it.
The town of it flooding in groves:
I drowned in a thousand dawns
To hear the doves.

To see the faces all alien
Standing along the track,
Watching the Flyer go by,
I looked back.

The place we loved was just a blur
We rubbed across the loam.
How soon the dirt and the earth close over
Above our home.

Barrett Canyon, California
August 28, 1946

"While one bird bears the noon . . ."

While one bird bears the noon
on a single note
and roofs the ferns with pools
from a singing throat,

While one pine holds the moon
on the mountainside
as it rolls across the world
toward its silver stride,

I flood over restfulness
like a town with groves
and gleam as a consequence
of all men's love.

Barrett Canyon, California
September 3, 1946

Like Ours

When I chopped the pine
    the staves ripped out of the pine.
    The splinters fell out of the years.

When I split the maple
    the curly beginnings of spring
    rippled away from the axe.

But when I struck the stunted oak
    it would not betray
    one year from the next.

It held all of its pitiful youth
    close in its heart.

Barrett Canyon, California
September 25, 1946

Humanity in the Service

The place by the ear
over the throat—
that's the place,
low note
and high regard.

There on your heroes
and heroines,
sweet and snow
and beautiful,
dressed to kill
in sober wool.

There's always a place on the uniform,
a place by the throat
where the purest wax
is warm.

Barrett Canyon, California
October 14, 1946

The Arrow Maker

heard the chipping
the careful sensation
time surprised in the flint
and hurried ten thousand years to a flake.

saw the stone
all the stone world
later made prison to sooner
and sprung only by chips, slow.

it rose in the throat
an arrow to startle today
a word pried from tomorrow—
all alone, jagged in time.

and poetry troubled the poet.

Barrett Canyon, California
November 3, 1946

Muttered Creed

Never again for any glorious thing
    stand in unison,
      or repeat after a leader
      or wear an award.
Always plead guilty.
Always say "Maybe."

Always expect everything—
	but land running, and headed for cover.
Always own a burrow somewhere.
Always know the line beyond which no retreat.
Have the speech ready.
Spring all the answers.
Retire to the mountains.
Barricade the canyon.
Loose the carrier pigeons.
Call out friendliness.
Knock on wood.
Offer to hew wood, carry water.
Greet the enemy.
Fall facing homeward
	and calling out clearly:
"Forgive!"

Barrett Canyon, California
December 3, 1946

Country Boy at College—Postwar

There was yearned—
	stamped over with pat pending
	copyright, permit, visa
	and please pay when served.

There were the flocks of teal
	smalling off beyond willow island
	and beating back upwind over the corn—
	snowed away by all these years.

There was the Rover, with his paws on goodness
    and his muzzle steadfast forever—
    proved weak through that strength,
    and a friend to even a fascist who would
    pat or give bones.

And there was whoever God was,
    holding up the sky, and always to lean on—
    taking orders from someone in the War Department.

Barrett Canyon, California
December 5, 1946

Members of the Kingdom

All over the world meeting briefly,
hunting fragile kingdoms like snow empires on the wind,
go a smoldering few whose eyes are smoke.
And often they call despair for their kind,
a grating of words across the rough of the world—
and then comes the polishing sound of their laughter,
baling the gust and building on the wind.

Barrett Canyon, California
December 6, 1946

Night Words

My hand invented sorrow,
shaped it round,
slowly with a finger smoothed it down,
then took it in the night
and hid it in the ground.

My ears heard sorrow moving,
then go still.
I leaned above the mound, sorrowful,
and held still time and breath.
Silence, too, can kill.

But now my hand is groping,
so still, so dumb,
hunting in the darkness, in the loam:
I have to find you, Sorrow.
Where you are is my home.

[Barrett Canyon, California]
1947

Smoke Trees

In the desert where no tree ought to grow
faintly over the valley rocks a few smoke trees,
without leaves, with hazy gray lacing branches,
leaned in the wind, puffs of gray, steadfast.

Coming out of any room after a day spent for money,
there over the mindscape faint and still
in front of every rock hard in the sunlight,
I see something light and unreal and enduring.

Barrett Canyon, California
January 2, 1947

At the Salt Marsh

Those teal with traveling wings
had done nothing to us but they were meat
and we waited for them with killer guns
in the blind deceitful in the rain.

They flew so arrowy till when they fell
where the dead grass bent flat and wet
that I looked for something after nightfall
to come tell me why it was all right.

I touched the soft head with eyes gone
and felt through the feathers all the dark
while we steamed our socks by the fire
and stubborn flame licked the bark.

Still I wonder, out through the raw blow
out over the rain that levels the reeds,
how broken parts can be wrong but true.
I scatter my asking. I hold the duck head.

Richmond, California
January 8, 1947

Those Few

They've gone.
Wide over,
    one after,
       two by.
Tuft by puff,
    raveled,
       slimmed away.
One morning open the eyes.
Where?

Put out hand.
Why?

Call out always:
    "Not even say goodbye!"

Barrett Canyon, California
February 8, 1947

Super Market

Every bit of yellow cheese in the market
    was wrapped in cellophane.
Every morsel of fruit was,
    every sprig of celery, every tomato.
All the prepared meat was in cellophane
    with a ribbon around it.

Around the room were clear troughs
    made of glass and chromium.
The neon sign rippled through glass.

Everyone in the market had on shined shoes,
    pressed clothes with cuffs and pleats.
The men all wore ties, wrapped over
    left to right, pulled up snug.
The women all had permanents;
    their mouths were coated with rouge.

When you carried your cellophaned food
    past the automatic adding machine
    and paid legal dollars and cents,
A girl said cellophaned thanks;
    the big machine added more dollars.
The bell rang, the line moved, the gate clicked;
    and you blinked out into darkness.

Barrett Canyon, California
February 15, 1947

Possession

Out of all reason rich,
out of all lifted and surged wealth,
out of all stormed-over gold and jewels,
I have a treasure.

It's a spark of darkness,
a nugget of night.
It's on the point of bone
where I turn my head.

Out of all reason precious,
no snow of Himalaya higher,
under the quietest current
of every day.

Never to be taken away,
my spark of darkness,
my own nugget of night.

Barrett Canyon, California
February 17, 1947

Veteran

I have jerked out of a fall
only to sink slow. . .
into the long, long groove of security.

I'm afraid of the peril of surety—
falling swoops down free and steep
but safety feels strange
and looks too deep.

Barrett Canyon, California
March 11, 1947

"There in the deep room . . ."

There in the deep room
    low past the lamps, shining,
I would reach back into time
And stop—near whom?

Not at the table by the hostess,
But there by someone lost.
I'd say, "Come at last,"
And whistle and softly laugh.

Say, "Sun grew. Sky squeezed. Earth thrust.
And here on the heart lay dust."

Remembering would come down
    like the late curlew
Through the pane of day
    and the shade of yesterday—
All that wonderful plastic—
To the place by the window
    in that deep room
    near you.

Barrett Canyon, California
March 20, 1947

Beginning of Hostilities

About here the sky goes under
    an extension of the earth
    painted like the sky.

The road goes into this tunnel
    painted like the sky
    and we never know.

Wide and then narrowing
    the low that looks high
    funnels into electric dimness.

Under the tunnel good people slide,
    adjusting their gloves and their rifles
    and pointing out the stars.

Barrett Canyon, California
April 10, 1947

Two Kinds of Faith

Some things I know hard,
the way a tree
near timberline
    believes the wind.

Some things I know easy,
the way long grass
meets autumn
    and says yes.

Barrett Canyon, California
April 12, 1947

"Your tears fell on my eyes . . ."

Your tears fell on my eyes
so near were we at night.
I saw the firelight
through your own lashes.

And laughter limpidly
streamed through your hair
and through the air
all stribbled fine.

Oh that was on the farm,
some other land
away from all this now—
you understand?

[Barrett Canyon, California]
May 20, 1947

Who Bow

Who bow like palms
in easy air
but rend a root
through rock
below the ground
are often still
at night
while sleep waits.

A greater visitor
than any boot
stamps at their door
and yet may knock—
and knocks,
and in the straight
sound of the clock
an easement starts.

Slow root through stone
push on
while brow of palm
will nod in pomp
until the moon
breaks all but still
lets nothing move or stop
except the brow, except the root.

Claremont, California
June 2, 1947

A Leader I Met

A leader I met
held through money a great power,
and he often let
corruption help him
stay great and become hoar.

When I touched him I felt
his lies peep out a hundred holes,

as if through cold fat
worms would start
and writhe out like blunt hair.

Claremont, California
June 28, 1947

The Materials

Square brick flat side straight face, clear, known,
fit here turn there on edge will do
up wall long tall stretch out reach on
no hole no break, like world fit true.

Then wait—last brick, have now but stone
round here bent there crack jag all through;
still turn still try move this one there
make yet straight wall, with stone—and care.

Claremont, California
July 3, 1947

Faint Message

This world, the chalice, held briefly the day,
Folded around it, knew with its wind the wall
Where I walked and met Alice, who has gone away.
We held the day, the wall, the wind stroking it all,

And we stood by the sea looking up far
Over the sharp edge where the islands fall
Tumbled a thousand miles. By the war
We parted, by its margin, and I have fallen
Down the war's flung sharp island years
To a shoal where I am pinned under debris:—
Ulysses' heavy bow, continents in tears,
And the cynical wind over the despondent sea.

Claremont, California
July 9, 1947

Relic

In the deep still wilderness
    lie comets
which fell, tearing leaves,
    and then lay silent.
What is this old cinder
    I heard drop
one day long ago
    and then forgot?

Claremont, California
July 25, 1947

Every Breakfast

Reading the morning news
    you look deep into a rifle
    with grooves down into the future
    where Mr. David Lilienthal
    and maybe some man from Congress
    and some kid reading the comics
    are making the trigger a prize.

Reading the morning news
    you look way down the grooves
    at the round lead slug that waits
    a single vote for bolt action
    to be the bullet future.

Reading the morning news
    you get those bulletin blues.

Claremont, California
August 2, 1947

Storm Warning

Something not the wind shakes along far
like a sky truck in low gear
over Oregon. Like the shore wind baying along through fir
but not now the wind, no, not really so,
it is a new weight and force
that begins to blow.

This winter they'll call it wind and let it explore;
and when they talk it over next summer there by the shore,
along through the scrub and salal the new something will range.
In a hurry, late, it won't wait for the air.

In the fall again they'll remember, each of them, back to now.
They'll no longer call it wind, they'll want it all changed.
They'll want it all different then, but they won't know how.

Claremont, California
August 22, 1947

The Verdict

Every day knows all but the dark rooms,
every night knows all but the neon;
half-shut eyes close around put questions,
then turn the day on.

Out, the eye looks every exit,
in, the pupil loads the tongue;
wide the mouth swings truth by the fingers,
and the jury's hung.

Driven spikes in the brain cry "Guilty!"
Dipped in circumstance lies fate.
The sky over both accused and the people
shines immaculate.

Claremont, California
August 28, 1947

Graduate Work

Perched there, footed on stone, up high,
reared the spare hall, packed with books and rooms.
Tile roofs and a cement wall kept mildew and rain
outside away from the sear parching turn
    of the leafed page.

Where my step grated on the drained floor
under a clear light sat a grim teacher,
reading Rabelais;
and when I bent for a drink at the tile fountain
    it was dry.

Berkeley, California
September 5, 1947

Sub-urban

In any town I must live near the rind,
where the animals come around nibbling.
Everything else inside may be designed,
but near is an edge, not confined.

They must be animals that, though mild,
come straying in only by night-time.
They don't belong, but come anyway, beguiled
by light, but ready to bolt for the wild.

That's how the wilds and I belong
around any kind of a city:

in front of us lights and all the glory and stir,
but back of us—country, as friendly as fur.

Berkeley, California
September 7, 1947

Postwar Niblets

The little table by the big entrance
    is for veterans.
If you can present a card
    you qualify for Heaven.
Though temporarily of course
    you are housed in Hell.

   . . .

First class you can't get any more.
What was second class is now first class.
What was third class is now second class.
What was fourth class is now third class.
Fourth class now is what we used to throw away.

   . . .

What there's a lot of, people don't want.
If you have it to sell, prices fall.
The costliest is what isn't at all.
    (But if you go down to the dump
    sometimes you can find silver
        thrown away.)

   . . .

"Some day the people will say 'No more war,'
    and there won't be any more."
"That's what I said last time—
    I refused to fight."
"Yes, that's all right, I guess—
    but what would have happened
    if we'd all been like you?"

Mill Valley, California
September 24, 1947

Inside Engines

There is no way to save the bearing.
Sliding parts will always wear.
If you make the joints open
The gasoline burns, but the piston won't care.

There is a strict justice around the valve grooves;
Nothing by halves, each turn of the cam effects a revolution;
The proletarian rings are warmly true—
But the worn gears run in a treacherous confusion.

All hail, however, the engine savior!
The opiate of the motor returns with unction.
The Christian oil forgives forever,
And the steadfast gauge gleams forth salvation.

Mill Valley, California
October 6, 1947

Too Big

The light things escape flying up;
the quiet ones hide near the ground;
those with long legs pull horizons
and run till the desert is brown.

Nothing is with me to stay.
All break or run out, pulling space.
They stretch the world big all around.
And I'm such a local place.

Mill Valley, California
October 7, 1947

Faith

If I could be,
   all alone,
   not held by the hand,
   nothing to make me know
   —just the turn of events,
   like so.
If I could alone decide,

I'd never deny.

Whatever was true
   I'd sing away at
   and never by dawn betray
   no matter the mist

no matter how gray
the shadow of wing of a bird.
I'd say each yea,

Even if saying were bad.

And somewhere below I'd expect
that connections be made.
And somewhere somehow that addition
of many times no
would mean okay.

Somehow, someday.

Berkeley, California
October 10, 1947

Outside

I touching the earth
outside the homes of great men
tangling the trees with my eyes—
how often their dogs recognized me
and their children and kine were afraid.

And yet what am I?
The weakest man.
The hobbling runner.
The gasping fighter.
The frightened stranger.

I stood there
touching the earth

tangling the trees with my eyes
being homeless and outside
frightening and afraid.

Richmond, California
October 17, 1947

The Myth of the Windblown Hair

There are tall in this town buildings
like trees with windows, and with
termited hollows all through the trunks.
To every door is a velvet path,

Or of tile or cement. Everyone, ox-eyed,
far-wandering, wise-hearted, child of wrath,
owns a stone tree, or a velvet path to a hollow.
And every excellence we have is a myth.

Above all, what we love—in leopard skin,
with rose, ever-blushing cheek, the always smile;
walking on elegant feet and a tilted eagerness;
within, a hinted slenderness and excellence full—

Each with the windblown hair, the shepherdess tan,
the captive bracelet and the captured charm—
everyone brave and modern, with newness on,
lapped in myths to keep us warm.

Berkeley, California
October 29, 1947

The Right Thing

Our great roar-wheel
shaking its weight
down the twin steel
crunches a bone
and leaves behind
under a stone,
leaning by fences—
somewhere along—
the right thing.

I thought it was only
Always, or something.
Maybe the Sky,
only the Sky.
But it was more:
It was the right thing.

Not at the station,
but back:
when they weren't looking.
When they were looking away.
Or when it was so big
they couldn't see.
That was the way.
It was like that.
We stayed aboard
and roared on by
the right thing.

Berkeley, California
November 18, 1947

It Was This Way

Again today I have not saved the world.
(My friends have been asking me to.)
But it took me so long to be neighbors
that while I was trimming my hedge
a war began between Arabs and Jews.

And off across the country my Congressman
dared 200,000,000 Russians to come over and fight.
Again today I have not saved the world.
And here it is, almost night.

Richmond, California
November 30, 1947

Credentials

Few folk around here have
      more leeries per *post hoc*
            than I have.

They are more easy come
      but also more easy go
            than I am.

Or perhaps it's in the *propter*—
      because they like to speak. . . .
            I'm a speak-low-doubter.

Richmond, California
December 4, 1947

Walking Papers

Foreman's house in the shade of a tree
owns a shack and a pretty daughter
richest man in the whole country
miles of view and a tank of water.

Hello, Mr. Foreman, hello Miss Daughter
just stopping by for a glass of water.

Felt thrown away like an old milk bottle
down on the cinders by the railroad track
walking papers in my pocket
sun shining down like a slap on the back.

Walking papers? why what do you mean
had a good job wherever I been.

Born in the shade of a water tank
in a town that owned a tree
an only child in an only town
in a wide and lone country.

So long, Mr. Foreman, so long, Miss Daughter
It's awful far to a glass of water.

Born in a town by a water tank
desert around the place
four long tracks to the end of the earth
distance touching my face.

Railroad jobs kept daddy poor
kids takes money and we got no more.

Walking papers in my pocket
left that town but never forgot
empty place in somebody's locket
steam in my heart like a coffee pot.

Richmond, California
December 6, 1947

Ruminations: Noon

Waited while he told the approved way.
Saw coming down like a mower through wheat
all the reasons he stood there and was great
while the jumped rabbits sat alert out in the weeds.

And the warehouse quality of it all
moved up over like a steel tent
until with a timid hunch I stopped and sat tall
and then wiggled my nose and began my lunch.

Soft and various as squirrels
I felt the little possibilities frisk out of the door
as I set down my ponderous heart
and began to beat.

Why have you carried it here for?
they jeered as they licked their teeth,
and I froze quite still in the stare of more and more
while I told everything please to wait.

Oh, there is no way quiet enough,
it is all running down, tomorrow is here.
As the clock snips the end off the lunch hour:
stand up, these are the days, and return to work.

Richmond, California
December 9, 1947

Rebel Telling You

We must cannot tell.
Necessary never done.
Obey, seldom well.
Compulsory always not.

Every neither meets.
Too bad goods all life.
Mend the knife that cuts,
break the breaker off.

Out by truly in,
Lowly meaning high,
always old begin,
looks like near the end.

Lightning easy slow
fragmented by all,
crack by weld we go
broken perfect whole.

Richmond, California
December 17, 1947

From the Back Row

Is the quiet note heard?
Does it richen the chord?

No one can hear it struck, low,
when they touch the bell once
near the end of the show.

The composer, though, heard it.
He wanted the bell.
He was rich, and could afford it.

It is not heard or counted, no.
No one can tell.
It is just *so.*

And there *is* something good about it.

Richmond, California
December 26, 1947

Wind Gift

For you, something not put
    even in prayer.
Like broad wings that swim thick
    under your fall
And won't let you drop
    through the air.

Or the same thing under the sea
    where your boat goes.
A teeming companionship
    of life too full for a hollow
—the way a canyon's alive
    when it snows.

That's the way, under and over
    and all around—
Miraculous out of the void
    All for you—
    so wild the eye roves
    wing, fin, flake
    nor touches the ground.

Richmond, California
December 27, 1947

"A million explosions went out . . ."

A million explosions went out
exploring as you talked
and I kept looking at the fire
steady and listening as the fuses
glowed and went out.

So far they echoed, repeated,
that I thought
maybe you would hear them
as they muffled me soft.

But I had to listen deeper
and ever deeper myself,
and I was listening so in the silence
that broke louder and louder
until you left.

Richmond, California
December 28, 1947

[Coda: A Dedication]

For no person
every glancing possibility in any person
for the times that harmonized
 briefly achieved, or that we may yet see—
and for a little dog that trotted
through the selective service office,
 January 7, 1942

Iowa City, Iowa
January 1952

Notes

For Poems—'42 and '43   (p. 3)
This poem was filed among Stafford's daily writings of 1944. Its title, however, suggests he had in mind the possibility of using it as a prefatory piece for some gathering of his poems from the previous two years.

1937–1941

White Pigeons   (p. 7)
At the bottom of the typescript is the following parenthetical notation: "(Written in study hall, the last semester at K.U. The first time I really tried to express poetry. Published in a little magazine in New Mexico.)" The poem, however, was not published in any literary journal, and it is not clear when the notation was composed, but "White Pigeons" does seem to be Stafford's first poem. The poem also presents the first of many issues in establishing final, stable texts. Stafford's capitalization of the first word in any given line is erratic in the typescript of this poem. There is evidence in the poem that he may have been experimenting with capitalization from the very start, but the evidence is not definitive. In addition, note that the absence of punctuation after "Soft" in line 18 seems intentional and expressive.

To Schumann-Heink   (p. 8)
Ernestine Schumann-Heink (1861–1936) was an operatic contralto who in her later years hosted a weekly radio program. This was Stafford's first published poem. *The Bard* (Jackson, Missouri), 5.3 (Fall 1938).

Purpose and *Subject and Background*   (pp. 8–9)
The Oread Magazine (March 15, 1941): 19 and 26, respectively. This was a literary magazine for University of Kansas students.

Communication from a Wanderer (pp. 9–12)
University Daily Kansan (May 14, 1941). This poem won the $100 first prize in the annual Carruth poetry contest. The epigraph is from the ending of Langland's *Piers Plowman,* and seems relevant to Stafford's future work and life. It is "Conscience" who speaks these words.

From the Sound of Peace (p. 12)
The Jayhawker (October 1941). A University of Kansas campus publication.

Home Town and *Women of Kansas* (pp. 15–16)
Feoh 1 (Spring 1942): 17. Another University of Kansas publication, with both poems published in 1942 but probably composed in Fall 1941.

Observation (p. 16)
Composed in "early December 1941," and published in *New Mexico Quarterly Review* 17 (Spring 1947): 84–85. Text printed here is from the poem's later revised publication in *New Signatures: A Selection of College Writing.* Allan Swallow, ed. Prairie City, IL: James A. Decker, 1947. 150. The anthology includes work by John Hollander and Flannery O'Connor, among others.

1942–1945

At Roll Call (p. 19)
Text of the poem, without the title, published in and used as epigraph for "Mountain Conscription," a chapter in *Down in My Heart.* Corvallis: Oregon State University Press, 2006. 68.

Event and *A Vine* (pp. 19–20)
Feoh 1 (Spring 1942): 34. These poems composed c. March 1942.

Buzzards over Arkansas (p. 21)
Text of the poem, without the title, published in and used as epigraph for "A Story From the Social Antennae," a chapter in *Down in My Heart.* 23.

CO Park Project (p. 23)
Poem also published in Kim Stafford's memoir, *Early Morning: Remembering My Father, William Stafford*. St. Paul: Graywolf Press, 2002. 85.

Los Prietos [I] (p. 28)
The three primary CPS camps Stafford was associated with were the following: Magnolia, Arkansas, from January 1942 to June 1942; Los Prietos, California, from June 1942 to May 1944; Belden, California, from May 1944 to February 1945. He was also in a variety of associated "spike camps," primitive worksites, usually with tents only. The main camps had barracks, mess halls, and running water. His last year in CPS was spent working for relief agencies connected to the Church of the Brethren. In the immediate aftermath of his service he continued to work for those agencies in the San Francisco Bay Area.

The Country of Thin Mountains (p. 29)
Motive 4 (May 1944). Later published in *Roving Across Fields: A Conversation and Uncollected Poems, 1942–1982*. Seattle: The Barnwood Press, 1983. 31.

Breath (p. 34)
Text of the poem, without the title, published in and used as epigraph for "We Built a Bridge," a chapter in *Down in My Heart*. 36.

CO's Work on Mountain Road (p. 36)
The Illiterati 2 (Summer 1943). This the literary journal published at the CPS camp at Wyeth, Oregon, and continued at Waldport, Oregon, a camp noted for its many artists, including the actor Kermit Sheets, the painter Kemper Nomland, the printers William Eshelman and Adrian Wilson, and the poet William Everson. This poem was later published in an *Anthology of Northwest Writing, 1900–1950*, edited by Michael Strelow and published by Northwest Review Books in 1979. Reprinted in 2003. The present text has been corrected by reference to Stafford's typescripts.

Search (p. 38)
The Illiterati 2 (Summer 1943).

Meditation (p. 38)
Poetry 71, in an earlier version. (November 1947): 71.

"We called it the chaparral..." (p. 40)
Text of the poem, without the title, published in and used as epigraph for "The Battle of Anapamu Creek," a chapter in *Down in My Heart*. 27.

"While we sat on the lawn..." (p. 44)
Composed at Manchester College, Indiana. This college was and still is affiliated with the Church of the Brethren. Stafford and other COs were sent there for a few weeks to help develop education and other administrative programs for the Brethren-based CPS camps. His letters report that a wide variety of pacifist speakers gave talks, and that in this "flavorable *(sic)* setting we have been living in spiritual luxury and meeting wonderful people." It was no doubt a welcome respite from the spike camps of Los Prietos.

Family Statement (p. 45)
Text used here published in *The Bridge*, 2.10 (July 20, 1948): 157–159. This has significant variations from an earlier version published in *Retort*, 2.1 (November 1943): 22. Glen Coffield, editor of *The Bridge*, noted that the later version he was publishing was printed from Retort, with recent modifications by the author, quoting Stafford as saying he would "modify it slightly—if not write a new poem today!" The *Retort* version of the poem is found in *Every War Has Two Losers*, Ed. Kim Stafford. Minneapolis: Milkweed Editions, 2003. 109–110.

Easy (p. 48)
The Illiterati 3 (Summer 1944).

More Than Bread (p. 50)
Text of the poem, without the title, published in and used as epigraph for "To Meet a Friend," a chapter in *Down in My Heart*. 85.

These Mornings (p. 52)
Every War Has Two Losers. 4.

Nocturne [II] (p. 53)
Ladies Home Journal 68 (June 1951): 132.

Devotion (p. 57)
Text of the poem, without the title, published in and used as epigraph for "Duet for Cello and Flute," a chapter in *Down in My Heart*. 73. The punctuation is that used in the collection *Winterward,* Stafford's PhD dissertation, University of Iowa, 1954.

To a Gold Star Mother (p. 58)
Fellowship 16 (October 1950): front cover.

"The One who said 'No violence'..." (p. 60)
Composed in Fredonyer Pass, one of the spike camps related to the Belden CPS camps. Others mentioned are Susanville, Gansner Bar, and Big Springs. These camps were in the Sierras northeast of San Francisco. Belden was the last of the main CPS camps to which Stafford was assigned.

Home (p. 63)
Text used here first published in *All about Light*. Athens, Ohio: Croissant and Company, 1978. In *Early Morning,* Kim Stafford used a text of this poem whose last two lines read as follows: "We had to sell the lock/ To own the star." These lines reflect handwritten revisions on the last typed draft. There is, however, no way to establish a stable and final authoritative text for this poem. The text used here reflects Stafford's later attitudes toward the poem. He seems to have gone back to to the words of the earliest draft of the poem, while somewhat altering the punctuation and capitalization.

Little Sermon (p. 64)
The Bridge 10.12 (December 1956). Later published in *Sometimes Like a Legend*. Port Townsend, WA: Copper Canyon Press, 1981.

Isaiah, '44 (p. 64)
New Mexico Quarterly Review 17 (Spring 1947): 84. Later published
in *New Signatures: A Selection of College Writing.* Allan Swallow, ed.
Prairie City, IL: James A. Decker, 1947. 149. Interestingly the poem is
there titled "Isaiah, '46," the date-change presumably to indicate the
poem's relevance to the post-war years. The typescript also indicates a
later change to "Isaiah, '54" and a later typescript has the title of "Isaiah,
'66," again presumably to indicate the poem's continuing relevance.

A Posy (p. 66)
Poetry 71 (November 1947): 70.

Speech from the Big Play (p. 68)
There is no archival indication that there ever was a big play that this
poem is drawn from. There is some indication that Stafford's sub-
title was possibly an alternative title, but the evidence for that is not
definitive.

Before the Big Storm (p. 71)
New Mexico Quarterly Review, 21.2 (Summer 1951) and *Traveling
through the Dark.* Evanston, IL: Harper & Row, 1962. 47.

The Tall Animals (p. 73)
New Orleans Poetry Journal 2.2 (April 1956): 2.

Footnote (p. 73)
Poetry 71 (November 1947): 70.

All White (p. 74)
The Oregonian. 1958. Later published in *Roving Across Fields:
A Conversation and Uncollected Poems, 1942–1982.* Seattle: The
Barnwood Press, 1983. 32.

Chicago Bridge, Evening (p. 75)
Composed at Elgin, Illinois, where the Church of the Brethren CPS program had its headquarters. Stafford was there from March 1945 to January 1946 when he was officially released from CPS.

The War Season (p. 78)
Stafford's note on typescript: "Published in *The Oregonian* in about 1948."

Twelve Years Old (p. 79)
Weather. Mt. Horeb, WI: Perishable P, 1969.

Mr. Conscience (p. 80)
Grundtvig Review 1 (Spring 1950).

Victory (p. 83)
Text of poem, without the title, published in and used as epigraph for "The End of the War," a chapter in *Down in My Heart.* 79.

Assay (p. 87)
Fellowship 14 (January 1948): 11. Collected in *A Scripture of Leaves.* Elgin, IL: Brethren Press, 1999. 17.

Review (p. 87)
Fellowship 13 (November 1947): 166.

1946–1947

To Those among Us Who Will Be Wise, and Know (p. 93)
Composed in Berkeley, California. After being released from CPS, Stafford taught high school and eventually went to work in the San Francisco Bay area for the Church World Service, a relief agency.

Two Bits Worth (p. 96)
Fellowship 16 (May 1950): 19.

So Long (p. 97)
Ladies Home Journal 67 (October 1950): 174.

Demolition Project (p. 100)
Tiger's Eye 1 (October 1947): 11. Later published in *Temporary Facts.*
Athens, OH: Duane Schneider, 1970.

Foundations (p. 100)
Fellowship 17 (January 1951): front cover. Poem composed in Glendale,
California. William and Dorothy Stafford had found teaching work in
southern California.

Home Town from the Flyer (p. 101)
Poem composed at Barrett Canyon, near Ontario, California.

Muttered Creed (p. 104)
Fellowship 13 (November 1947): 166.

Members of the Kingdom (p. 106)
Often used as a colloquial name for COs from the CPS camps.

Night Words (p. 107)
Fiddlehead (Fall 1958): 21. Earlier version in *Winterward,* Stafford's PhD
dissertation at the University of Iowa, 1954.

At the Salt Marsh (p. 108)
West of Your City. Los Gatos, CA: Talisman Press, 1960. 14.

Those Few (p. 109)
Tuft by Puff. Mt. Horeb, WI: Perishable Press, 1978. Also published in
The Oregonian, c.1950.

Super Market (p. 109)
Poetry 73 (October 1948): 19.

Two Kinds of Faith (p. 113)
Arizona Quarterly 4 (Autumn 1948): 202.

Faint Message (p. 116)
Poetry 71 (November 1947): 71.

Storm Warning (p. 118)
Rough Weather 1 (Fall 1950). Collected in *Sometimes Like a Legend*. Port Townsend, WA: Copper Canyon Press, 1981. 49.

Sub-urban (p. 120)
Sometimes Like a Legend. 9.

It Was This Way (p. 127)
Fellowship 14 (July 1948): 12.

Credentials (p. 127)
North by West, with John Haines. Karen Sollid and John Sollid, eds. Seattle: Spring Rain Press, 1975. 35.

Walking Papers (p. 128)
Ladies Home Journal 70 (October 1953): 100.

Acknowledgments

The William Stafford Archive, presently in Portland, Oregon, has been directed by Paul Merchant for the past ten years. Mentioning him in this paragraph in no way captures the degree to which his assistance has made this book possible. Stafford was enormously well-organized in saving his correspondence, his daily writing, his typescript copies, and many of his publications, but his diligent organization often increased the number of variables later at play when we began to assemble for publication a collection of materials from the Archive. In preparing this book, we also had to cope with the fact that there are no handwritten versions of Stafford's poetry before 1950. Stafford preserved only typescript versions of the poems. Due in some part to the exigencies of his life in the CPS camps, the typescript was on sheets of 8½ by 5½ inches. This made for neatness and portability, and a paper size that Stafford found useful throughout his life, especially when he traveled and gave readings.

Nevertheless, paper of this size presented him with problems when it came to lineation. Stafford often experimented with a longer line than one might expect. Thus on these typescript versions of the poems, lines of poetry were frequently broken and indented because of space limitations. In reading them, it is sometimes obvious that one is dealing with a space issue, but sometimes not. Stafford was just as likely to experiment with a short line and use indentation as an expressive device. Often one had to make reasonable inferences as to whether a given indentation was forced upon the author by virtue of the page size, or whether he was choosing a certain a new line-length and spacing. Similar, though easier editorial judgments had to be made in regard to handwritten, interlineated revisions, and in regard to his punctuation and capitalizations. Sometimes the most difficult editorial judgments, however, involved the multiple versions of individual poems, wherein one needed to discern which version of the text was most reliable and most fully intended. Scores of poems from 1937–1947 exist in multiple typescript or published versions, and each had to be evaluated. In all these tasks, Paul Merchant was enormously insightful, exceptionally generous, and unfailingly helpful. When Paul became the director, he built upon the invaluable work of Vincent and Patty Wixon, who had helped Kim Stafford establish the Archives. All three have been unstinting in their devotion to the work of William Stafford. All readers and researchers who have ever visited the Archives owe Paul Merchant, and Vincent and Patty Wixon, a profound debt of gratitude.

This project began in the William Stafford Archives, around a small wooden table where I sat across from Kim Stafford. I had worked with Kim before, first on the editorial process involved in his assembling *The Way It Is*, and then later as an editorial reader of *Early Morning*, his memoir about his father. Kim is the executor of his father's estate, a stewardship that he accomplishes with grace, devotion, good will, and the sure sense that his father's skillful ways of balancing life and writing are a model for us all, especially as we do this work of legacy. Whenever and wherever I would meet with Kim, his first question was not about the project involving his father's poetry, but always about how well my own writing was going. For the opportunity to undertake this project, for the buoyant affirmations throughout the process, and for the friendship at the heart of it all, I thank you, Kim. And if one wants to know at least one source of Kim Stafford's affirmations, one need only look to his mother, Dorothy, who along with the rest of the Stafford family, welcomed me as a friend. For that, and for the abiding sparkle of your thought, I thank you, Dorothy.

In addition to Paul Merchant, the Director of the Archives, I want to thank Diane McDevitt, Archive Assistant, who opened her home to me when I journeyed to Portland, and who, along with her partner Scott, created a rose garden adjacent to the Archives, a fragrant space that allowed one to ease into the day's research, thought, and writing. I also want to thank Doug Erickson, the Director of the Lewis and Clark College Archives, and a true friend of William Stafford and this project. At the other end of the country I want to thank my colleagues in the English Department at Suffolk University in Boston, especially Tony Merzlak, Deanna Stanford, Bette Mandl, and Jenny Barber, each of whom listened with care to the stories of this project as it unfolded. I also want to thank my friend and colleague James Carroll, himself a great teacher about the nature of conscience. I especially want to acknowledge the Dean of the College of Arts and Sciences, Kenneth S. Greenberg, whose support made my journeys to the Stafford Archives possible, and whose friendship continually illuminates and deepens my understanding of what it means to be an educator.

I am delighted to thank Ms. Fiona McCrae, Mr. Jeff Shotts, and Ms. Katie Dublinski, all of Graywolf Press. Friends it was your vision that started this work, and your vision that sustains it.

Finally, I want to thank my wife and life-partner, Stefi Rubin. Only you know the thousand ways you have made this work possible.

WILLIAM STAFFORD (1914–1993) after the war taught high school English, worked for Church World Service, and eventually joined the English faculty at Lewis and Clark College in Portland, Oregon, where (with time out for earning a PhD from the University of Iowa) he taught until his retirement. He authored sixty-seven books. His first book of poetry, *West of Your City,* was published when he was forty-six. In addition to the 1963 National Book Award for *Traveling through the Dark,* Stafford's many honors included serving as Poetry Consultant for the Library of Congress (1970–71) and winning the Shelley Award from the Poetry Society of America. He was appointed Oregon Poet Laureate in 1975. A generous mentor to aspiring poets everywhere, Stafford traveled thousands of miles giving hundreds of readings in colleges, universities, community centers, and libraries throughout the United States and beyond.

FRED MARCHANT is the author of three books of poetry. *Tipping Point* won the 1993 Washington Prize from The Word Works, Inc. *Full Moon Boat* was published by Graywolf Press in 2000, and *House on Water, House in Air: New and Selected Poems* was published by Dedalus Press of Dublin, Ireland in 2002. He is also the co-translator (with Nguyen Ba Chung) of *From a Corner of My Yard,* poetry by the Vietnamese poet Tran Dang Khoa. He is Professor of English and the Director of the Creative Writing Program, and Co-Director of the Poetry Center at Suffolk University in Boston. In 1970 he became one of the first officers ever to be honorably discharged as a conscientious objector from the United States Marine Corps. His new book of poetry, *The Looking House,* is forthcoming, also from Graywolf Press, in 2009.

Another World Instead has been typeset in Warnock Pro, an Adobe Originals font designed by Robert Slimbach. Book design by Wendy Holdman. Composition by BookMobile Design and Publishing Services. Manufactured by Maple Vail Book Manufacturing on acid-free paper.